About the Author

Theresa Cheung was born into a family of psychics and spiritualists. Since gaining a Masters from King's College, Cambridge, she has been involved in the serious study of the paranormal for over 25 years and has been a student of the College of Psychic Studies in London. She is the author of a variety of books including the international bestseller *The Element Encyclopedia of 20,000 Dreams* as well as *The Element Encyclopedia of the Psychic World, The Element Encyclopedia of Birthdays* and *Working with Your Sixth Sense.* Her books have been translated into 20 different languages and her books and writing have featured in *It's Fate, Spirit and Destiny* and *Prediction* magazines. She has also worked on books for Derek Acorah, Yvette Fielding and Tony Stockwell.

Theresa believes *An Angel Called My Name* was born in answer to her own questions and as a gift to herself and others. She has a great interest in angels, spirit guides, dreams and visions of the afterlife and feels that the angels are guiding and directing her writing and her life. She has also had several angel experiences herself, some of which she shares here.

If you have had an angel experience and wish to share it with Theresa she would love to hear from you. Please contact her, care of HarperElement, Editorial Department, 77–85 Fulham Palace Road, London W6 8JB or email any inspiring and uplifting stories direct to her at angeltalk710@aol.com.

An Angel
called my name

An Angel called my name

Incredible true stories from the other side

Theresa Cheung

HarperElement
An Imprint of HarperCollins*Publishers*
77–85 Fulham Palace Road,
Hammersmith, London W6 8JB

The website address is: www.thorsonselement.com

and *HarperElement* are trademarks of
HarperCollins*Publishers* Ltd

First published by HarperElement 2008

1 3 5 7 9 10 8 6 4 2

A catalogue record of this book is
available from the British Library

ISBN-13 978-0-00-727713-1
ISBN-10 0-00-727713-X

Printed and bound in Great Britain by
Clays Ltd, St Ives plc

Contents

Introduction:
The Voice of an Angel

The guardian angels of life sometimes fly so high as to be beyond our sight, but they are always looking down upon us.

Jean Paul Richter

I have always believed in the afterlife. I believe that loved ones watch over us from the other side and that guardian angels, or spiritual guides, walk with us through the journey of our life. I also believe that guardian angels can manifest themselves in countless miraculous ways. They may appear as a bird, a feather, a child, a puff of air, a gentle touch, a song on the radio, a coincidence, a dream, a mysterious scent, a flash of insight, or in other people who are consciously or unconsciously guided by those from a spiritual dimension.

My earliest recollection of forming an intense connection with the afterlife began at the age of four or five when my great aunt Rose told me to always save part of my seat for my guardian angel. It makes me smile even now as I remember shuffling forward in my seat to make room for an invisible guest without hesitation or doubt.

In the years that followed – although I did eventually stop shuffling forward every time I sat down – I never lost my belief that an angel was always at my shoulder. My family was constantly on the move and I never got opportunities to build lasting friendships at the various schools I attended, but I never felt lonely. Why should I be? My angels were constantly with me.

Looking back it's no surprise that great aunt Rose's words made a lasting impression on me. Although she died just before my tenth birthday, I remember her vividly as an independent and impressive lady with a twinkle in her brilliantly blue eyes. Growing up at the turn of the century, Rose's decision to devote her life to the work of a professional medium raised many an eyebrow among her peers – even though spiritualism was all the rage at the time. It was common place for séances to be held in church halls and private homes and Rose's mediumistic skills were much in demand. During both World Wars she was a source of hope, comfort and healing to those who lost loved ones.

I had the privilege to watch my great aunt in action on just one occasion when she agreed to give a rare public demonstration. I was very young at the time, and most of the details of what transpired at this gathering have faded from my memory, but I do recall how electric the atmosphere was.

One of my remaining memories from the demonstration is that of Rose telling a recently bereaved widower in the audience that the spirit of his wife was standing right behind him with her hand on his left shoulder. The man shook his head in disbelief. Rose told him that his wife had always wanted to hold hands in public but he had never let her and it would be healing for both of them to hold hands now. The man nodded in surprised agreement and admitted that holding hands in public had never been his style during their 20-year marriage. Encouraged by Rose he gently raised his left hand to his left shoulder and caressed invisible fingers. I remember looking at him and wondering, as only a child can, how it was possible to have tears in your eyes and a smile on your face at the same time.

Rose wasn't the only medium in my family. My grandmother, mother and brother were all born with the gift. My grandmother could not only see spirits but she also had the uncanny ability to know exactly what people were thinking and feeling; a gift inherited by my mother who earned her living as a psychic counsellor and my brother who also worked in the field.

Obviously, talk of sensing, feeling and communicating with spirits was commonplace in a family like mine.

There were, of course, embarrassing moments – like when my mother told my first boyfriend to stop seeing my best friend behind my back because the spirits were watching (she was right, as mothers usually are) – but there were also magical moments – like the time my brother told our neighbours exactly where their missing and much loved dog was.

When you consider that I was born into a family of psychics, my unshakeable conviction that there is an afterlife isn't surprising. However, it is surprising when you consider that until my mid-thirties I never actually received any personal evidence of the existence of angels or spirits.

I didn't levitate in my cot or see dead people in the school playground. At college I couldn't read my tutor's mind and later in life I often couldn't tell the difference between intuition and fear. I couldn't talk to angels or sense when spirits were present and my dreams, although surreal and colourful, were never precognitive or particularly illuminating. In fact, I was completely normal – if there is such a thing as normal. I had a wealth of anecdotal evidence from people I loved and trusted but I had certainly not inherited the gift. In fact, I was often gently teased by family and friends for my inability to make contact; my brother had great fun calling me 'square head'.

Despite the light-hearted teasing I never felt jealous or anxious that I couldn't sense, hear or see the spirits and angels like the rest of my family. In my mind I simply accepted that encountering an angel is extremely rare and that even though the angels weren't connecting, speaking or appearing to me they were still watching and guiding me. And if truth were told I was secretly relieved they didn't reveal themselves directly to me as I openly admitted to moments of fear. Like many people who share an interest in the spiritual side of life, I didn't actually need or want proof that angels and spirits exist, or even think proof was necessary. I was content to observe and believe in the psychic world that held me spellbound rather than experience it first hand.

Little did I know that, at the age of 33, all this would change!

Take the Right Path

About ten years ago, when I was living and working as a journalist in Dallas, Texas, I had a vivid dream. In this dream my mother was calling my name and telling me – just like she always used to do whenever I felt anxious or afraid – to follow my intuition as it would lead me to the right path in life. When I woke up I lingered in bed longer than usual reliving the dream in my mind's eye. My mother had passed away a decade previously and I missed her wisdom and warmth greatly. She had always told me to follow my heart and I silently promised her that even though I was working in journalism now I wouldn't give up on my dream of establishing myself as a writer of books.

That afternoon a radio interview was scheduled for me to talk about a series of articles I was writing for the local newspaper about ordinary people whose lives had been touched by the extraordinary. I was running late and as I leapt into the car to drive to the studio I soon realized that if I was to get there on time I would need to put my foot down. All was going well on the roads until I got stuck behind two massive trucks travelling at what seemed like 30 miles an hour. They were probably going much faster than that but when you are in a hurry every vehicle in front seems slow. I tried to overtake but couldn't get a clear view of the oncoming traffic so had to settle for a frustratingly slow crawl.

Finally, we reached a junction and I had a clear choice. I could turn left and follow the trucks along a shorter route and reach the studio in the nick of time or I could turn right, free myself from the trucks and take a longer route and possibly end up a few minutes late. I was just about to turn left and chug slowly along behind the trucks in front until I reached my destination when out of nowhere my dream flashed into my mind's eye. Once again I saw my mother calling my name and gently telling me to take the right path. Without hesitation, and not really understanding why, I turned right and predictably turned up at the studio late. I missed my radio interview. The network didn't have another slot to schedule me in.

As I drove back that day I felt frustrated and angry at a missed opportunity and time wasted. I got even more irritated when the traffic slowed to a crawl and then a halt. My irritation soon turned to horror when I gradually edged closer to the scene of what was clearly a terrible accident. Close to the junction where I had turned right the truck I had been following had clearly swerved off the road. Three or more cars – it was hard to tell in the chaos – had smashed into the truck and each other. The car immediately behind it – which would have been my car – was a mangled wreck and the two cars behind that also looked like smashed and battered.

Later that evening, I turned on the television to hear the local news. Images of the accident flashed onto the screen. A stray dog had run into the road in between the first and second truck. The second truck driver had slammed on the brakes and caused a pile up. Although the lorry driver and the dog were unharmed there were two passengers in the car immediately behind, a recently married couple called Jane and Harry, and one in the car behind that, a retired postal worker called Sam. All three had died on impact.

By telling me to take the right path, the voice of my mother had saved my life that day. I had not expected to ever find proof of an afterlife, but I had been given it all the same through a dream and a sudden flash of intuition. But instead of feeling elated by my experience, nothing seemed to make sense to me at all. All I could think was, 'Why should I be alive and not those poor people?'

Emotionally drained, I fell into bed that night to wake in the small hours of the morning from a restless sleep. My pillow was on the floor and the sheets and bedcovers had been pulled off the edge of the bed. 'What did it all mean?' I prayed. So many emotions clashed inside of me – the gratitude for living, the pain of hearing that people had died and the guilt of still being alive when they weren't. Why did they have to die? Why wasn't it me instead? Where were these people now? Were they all right? Still pleading for answers I fell back to sleep.

It was a voice that woke me. I heard a voice, a whisper really, calling my name. At first I thought it was my mother's voice. I sat up and looked around my bedroom but no one was there. Then I heard the voice again. 'Don't feel afraid. My name is Jane and I am all right. Everything is all right for us and everything will be all right for you too.'

And that was it. The voice was gone. I only heard it for a few seconds but it was just long enough to affect the rest of my life. A feeling of peace and comfort came over me, a feeling I had not known before like a warm, soft and luxurious blanket wrapped all around my body.

I pinched myself and it hurt. I was awake. I had heard the voice. This was real. I got up and turned the light on and the feeling of peace, the comfort of knowing everything would be all right continued to envelop me. My prayer had been answered. I still didn't know why my life had been miraculously spared on the day before but I did know that Jane and the other two people who died were okay. And I felt a new resolve to live a life that would make those who died instead of me in that terrible accident proud.

Simply Believing

Just as angels can appear in various guises, everyone connects with them in their own unique way. Some people are blessed with the rare ability to see or hear angels, or the spirits of those who have passed on, but it is more common to smell an essence, hear a familiar sound or simply sense a shift in energy or feeling. More common still – and my experience seven years ago may fall in this category – are revealing dreams, meaningful coincidences, subtle signs, flashes of insight and those little whispers, voices, inspirations and understandings we hear that encourage, comfort, guide or support us through life.

It is difficult to prove to someone the existence of angels since most of us can't touch or even see them, but this lack of proof only seems to be a problem to those who don't believe. To those who do believe there is no need to prove something they already know with absolute certainty.

Angels can occasionally appear uninvited in times of grief and danger to both believers and non-believers, but more often than not we need to let our angels know we are open to their help before they speak to us. Simply believing in them is really all that it takes to invoke the love and guidance of angels into our hearts and our lives. Our belief lets them know we want their guidance and we want them to be a part of our lives. Our belief is what lifts the veil between this life and the next.

Save a Seat for Your Angel

In this book I want to share with you just some of the thousands of compelling true stories I have collected from people whose lives have been touched and transformed by angels over the 25 years I have been researching and writing features, books and encyclopaedias about spirits, ghosts, dreams and the psychic world. The stories range from the inspirational to the comforting to the spine tingling, but despite varying widely in content they all have one thing in common: they are all real-life stories based in fact not fantasy.

I'd like to begin our psychic journey together, though, with some more of my own experiences. I hope that understanding a little more about me and what I have experienced and continue to experience every day will help you get to know me a little better.

I'm a 40-something married mum of two children; my son is ten and my daughter is eight. Although astonishing things have happened in my life – and I hope they will continue to happen as nothing fascinates or delights me more – I'm not a psychic, a medium or a spiritual guru. I do believe, however, that we are all born psychic in one way or other and there are times in our lives when we can tap into this. Many unusual things that I have experienced have been tied up with my work as a paranormal writer, which has encouraged me to reach out and explore the world of spirit, but other things have simply 'happened'. By sharing my personal psychic journey with you in the first chapter I hope you'll see that anyone, whatever their age or background, can hear the voice of an angel.

The rest of the book explores some of the incredible 'angel stories' I've encountered over the years. I'm extremely grateful to all those people who allowed me to interview them and gave me permission to share their experiences and their integrity. A few sent in their own versions of their experiences but in most cases I have written up their stories from what I was told or sent. Everyone who contributed touched me deeply with their truth and honesty.

Many of the people I spoke to were extremely relieved to tell their stories, sometimes for the first time. They wanted them included to show others that angels are always with us, even if we can't see them. Although names, dates and personal details have been changed at the request of those who wished it, the true accounts from ordinary people show just some of the many different ways those who pass on can reach back into our world. At the end of the day they are all heavenly stories that bring simple messages of support, hope, reassurance and love through angelic encounters and angelic words that transform this life and offer tantalizing glimpses of the next.

As momentarily unsettling as encounters with spirits and angels can be, especially to those who were previously unaware or unconvinced of their existence, I can assure you that the more I've learned and continue to learn about the world of spirit, the more comforting, wonderful and fascinating they become – and you will find that the same is true for you.

So save a seat for your angel and prepare to be inspired and astounded – as I never fail to be – by the true stories of people leading outwardly normal lives, but who have been comforted, inspired and transformed by the voice of an angel. Working on this book has opened my eyes to new paths and possibilities and given me a renewed connection to the realm of spirit. It is my sincere wish that reading it will serve as a catalyst for your own belief by proving to you that miracles can happen and that even ordinary people, like you and me, can wake up one day and hear an angel call their name.

May angels rest beside your door,
May you hear their voices sing.
May you feel their loving care for you,
May you hear their peace bells ring.
May angels always care for you,
And not let you trip and fall.
May they bear you up on angel's wings,
May they keep you standing tall.
May they whisper wisdom in your ear,
May they touch you when you need,
May they remove from you each trace of fear,
May they keep you from feeling greed.
May they fill you with their presence,
May they show you love untold,
May they always stand beside you
And make you ever bold.
May they teach you what you need to know
About life here and here-after.
May they fill you always with their love
And give you the gift of laughter.

Anon

An Angel
called my name

CHAPTER 1

Birth of an Angel

Death is no more than passing from one room into another. But there's a difference for me, you know. Because in that other room I shall be able to see.

Helen Keller (blind and deaf from infancy)

'I want an epidural!' I screamed harshly. 'I need an epidural and I need it NOW.'

I was being wheeled into the delivery room and the only thing on my mind was getting that epidural. I'd had an epidural for my son's birth. His entrance into the world had been blissfully calm and peaceful. While I was in 'labour' with him I'd even managed to get a few hours' sleep. Then I'd had a tranquil hour or so mentally to prepare myself before he was ready to be born. There had been no pain and no screaming; just a perfect birth.

Things couldn't have been more different second time round! My daughter had decided to make her grand entrance into this world a good ten days before her due date. She was in a hurry. By the time I got to hospital there was no time for an epidural or anything. This didn't stop me screaming for one until my voice was hoarse. The pain was out of this world.

'Take some deep breaths. Try to stay calm,' the doctor urged. I wanted to kill him! My husband held my hand. He told me to breathe deeply. I wanted to kill him too! My pain threshold has always been really, really low. I'm terrified of dentists and injections and I faint at the sight of my own blood. Giving birth without pain relief was my nightmare scenario made real. The more I tried to stay calm and breathe deeply the more panicked and tense I got.

'You are making things harder for yourself than they need to be,' I heard my doctor say. Or was it my mother?

Suddenly, I was five years old again. My mum was tucking me up in bed. I'd woken up screaming in the middle of the night. I was convinced there was a creature in my room. I pointed to the shadows to make my mum look. My mum smiled and brushed the hair away from my face. She told me that the presence I'd sensed in my room was my guardian angel looking down on me. There was nothing to be afraid of. She kissed me and I wasn't afraid any more.

I opened my eyes. I was back in the delivery room. My mum had passed away years ago but now with my eyes open I could still hear her calm and reassuring voice speaking clearly. I could feel the warmth of her breath. She told me to stop fighting and meet the challenge peacefully. I could feel her holding my hand. I listened to what she was whispering and began to take deep breaths. I started to calm down and instead of fighting the pain I distanced myself from it. Soon the hurt gradually faded away into nothing. I felt light and carefree. My beautiful daughter was born about 20 minutes later. I didn't feel any pain at all. Her birth was as blissful and calm as that of my gorgeous son – but this time the voice of my mother in spirit, and not drugs, had helped me through the pain.

Looking back I can see that throughout my life I have had many similar experiences which can be described as unusual; astonishing even. It's only recently, though, that I have been able to look back and recognize them for what they were.

Although my mother was a psychic counsellor and my grandmother a medium, not all of my early life was spent attending séances and reading tarot cards. I spent a great deal of it doing ordinary things that all children do. My dad couldn't work because he was disabled and we relied on my mum's income, which was minimal and unpredictable. Money was always tight, but somehow it didn't seem to matter. We never placed great value on material things and we always managed to have enough to eat and a roof over our heads. We couldn't afford holidays and treats but trips to the seaside and park were always part of our routine.

There is one park visit I remember very clearly. I was about six at the time. I can see myself now playing happily with my brother on the seesaw while my mother read a book on a bench nearby. It was a lovely day, the first of the school summer holidays. Suddenly, I started to feel very sick. I got off the seesaw and the sickness passed but when I got back on the seesaw I started to feel sick again. I loved the seesaw and hadn't felt sick like this when I was on it before. Stubbornly I tried to stay on. The feeling got worse. I could almost feel the vomit in my throat and taste it in my mouth. I had to admit defeat and decided to get off and play on the swings instead.

A little girl and her older sister squealed with delight when my brother and I got off. I watched them enviously from the swing as they went up and down. I swung higher and higher on my swing, trying to convince myself that I was having more fun. I wasn't. I didn't feel sick any more and toyed with the idea of demanding the seesaw back. It was my favourite thing to do in the playground.

I stopped swinging so hard so that I could easily jump off, but as I did I realized that the younger girl on the seesaw wasn't laughing anymore, she was crying. Her sister hadn't noticed and was bouncing higher and higher. The more the little girl cried, the harder her sister bounced. She only stopped when her little sister started to vomit. The father of the two girls ran over to comfort his vomiting daughter but now she was choking on her vomit. He screamed for help and his wife or girlfriend ran to a phone box. (This was in the days before mobile phones, remember.) The girl had passed out by the time the ambulance arrived and she was rushed to hospital.

Later we found out that the little girl made a full recovery. I was thrilled not just for her but, rather selfishly, also for me. I hadn't told my mum or my brother about my feelings of sickness on the seesaw. If something terrible had happened to her I was worried they would really be angry with me for not warning the little girl in time.

Warning or advising people was something my mother was highly skilled at. She had inherited the gift of psychic awareness and was an uncannily accurate astrologer/psychic counsellor. She'd give readings for people and wasn't afraid to give them advice, even advice they didn't want to hear. Once she told a bride-to-be that it might be a good idea to postpone her wedding. When the woman asked why my mum wasn't able to give her specifics but she was convinced that it would be a bad move. The woman was furious and said she never wanted to see my mother again for a reading. The wedding went ahead as planned. Sadly, the wedding was revealed as a sham four months later when the bride found out that her husband already had a wife!

5

I longed to be able to know and say clever things like my mother. I wanted to be able to help or warn people like she did. There was the odd difficult situation, like that of the unfortunate bride mentioned above, but most people who came to my mum for a reading were extremely grateful for her guidance and insight. Trying to copy my mum, I read every book I could lay my hands on from Dion Fortune to Colin Wilson. By the age of 14 I was something of an expert in the psychic arts. Tarot cards and numerology were my specialist areas. I got so good at on-the-spot readings with just a person's name for reference and a pack of tarot cards that my mum arranged for me to read at a local psychic fair. I read for over 20 people that day but afterwards I felt unworthy. I refused to accept the money I had earned. What I had was a good memory and knowledge from books. The readings I had given that day were based on my intimate knowledge of the theory of numerology and tarot card spreads. I hadn't had any blinding insights of my own. I hadn't inherited the gift. I wasn't psychic ... yet!

I talked to my mother about my concerns and she was happy for me to stop reading professionally. She told me that I needed time to grow and find my true talents. I felt keenly that I had disappointed her and let her down because I wasn't really psychic and couldn't see spirits and my brother could. I was determined to change that.

I signed up for a number of psychic development courses. Soon I was a walking expert on techniques to nurture your intuition and exercises to develop your psychic powers. My mum repeatedly offered to help me but I told her that this was something I had to do by myself. I made progress but not as much as I would have liked. My tutor at the College of Psychic Studies once told me that he thought I was trying too hard. What I needed to do was relax. I didn't agree with him. I'd always been told by my grandmother that anything was possible if you worked hard enough and wanted something enough. Besides, I was a tense and stubborn teenager; relaxing was one thing I really couldn't do.

I wanted to see, hear or feel angels so desperately, but after a couple of years it was like bashing my head against a brick wall. I was getting nowhere. Frustrated at my lack of progress and disillusioned with myself, I decided that it might perhaps be time to focus my energies elsewhere. It was time to get real, get some qualifications and a career.

I was 17 by now. Going back to sixth form was out of the question as my O level results had been dismal, so I enrolled on a home correspondence course to do my A levels. For the next two years I studied by myself at home. A lot of people, in particular my old school teachers and headmistress, thought it was a crazy idea. But what they hadn't accounted for was my discipline and will power. I was going to prove them all wrong. And prove them wrong I did.

People always say that school is the best time of your life but it certainly wasn't for me. I hated school. It wasn't until I began to study alone, free from the distraction of register taking, playground politics and a one-size-fits-all approach to education that I actually got a passion for learning. I wouldn't recommend this approach to everyone, but for me it was perfect.

To contribute to the household bills while I was studying the only job I could find was as an evening and weekend part-time care assistant at a local old people's home. You might think it's an odd place for a teenager to choose to work, but I didn't mind at all. Many young people feel nervous or bored around the elderly but it was the opposite for me. I felt very comfortable. I loved their wisdom and their experience. However ill, frail, confused or infirm they were, I always saw light in their eyes. In my mind's eye I could see the children they once were, full of energy and laughter.

Anyone who has ever worked in an old people's home will know that death is part of the routine. I wasn't unsettled by it. The first time I saw a dead body I felt a deep sense of peace. I also felt strangely detached from the body as it was clear from looking at it that the spirit had long gone. The body left behind reminded me of clothes that weren't going to be worn anymore. I also found that I could usually tell which resident was close to passing. It wasn't anything to do with their physical health. A day or so before they died the light in their eyes started to fade. The child that I imagined them to be in my mind was waving goodbye.

Seeing people so close to the end of their lives encouraged me to make the most of mine. I studied hard and surprised everyone, including myself, when I ended up with a place at Cambridge University reading English and Theology. I think the university liked the fact that I had not followed the same well-trodden path as everyone else. (Oh, the delight in writing to my old school and proving all the doubters wrong!) What I hadn't anticipated when I finally arrived was how hard it was to fit in at a place of such tradition and learning if you come from a low-income family – and an alternative family at that.

Two weeks into my first term I had my bags packed all ready to go home. I was going to tell my family that I wouldn't be going back. I didn't think I was up to it. I just didn't fit in. I was out of my league. I didn't have the clothes, the confidence or the money. In those days I was fortunate enough to be given a full grant but even the financial relief wasn't enough to make me want to stay. It was during this period in my life that my dreams first began to speak to me loud and clear. The night before heading home I had a dream in which I heard a choir of angels singing. Their voices and the song they sang was so piercing and enchanting that it stayed with me as I woke up the next morning. I could still hear every clear note of it in my head.

After breakfast I went to my pigeonhole and collected my post. I had a train to catch and was running late so I stuffed everything in my bag and got a bus to the station. Nobody was in when I eventually arrived home. For reasons I can't explain I hadn't wanted to phone in advance to warn my mum I was leaving. I went into my bedroom to unpack.

A brown envelope fell out of my bag, along with the rest of my college post. I ripped the envelope open and found a tape inside. It was a choral classic collection sung by the choir of King's College, Cambridge. There was no note or explanation, just the tape. Intrigued, I decided to play it and as soon as the first track began I recognized the song I had heard in my dream. The singing sounded more grounded than the tones I had heard in my dream but the piece was almost the same. It was called 'Miserere Mei, Deus'. (If you've never heard this choral piece you're missing out on something very special. It's incredibly inspiring and uplifting.)

I realized then that the angels had sent me this dream to remind me that I had been given a wonderful opportunity to study. I shouldn't let low self-esteem or fear of failure blow my chances. I repacked my bag and travelled back that same day.

It took a good term or two to find my feet but I stayed strong even when I found my belief in the afterlife seriously challenged by academics and men and women of learning. Eventually, though I began to feel as if I belonged and the next few years of my life were a blur of study and more study – and the odd party, debate, play and drink or two. But I did finish my degree and it helped me land my first job working as an editorial assistant for the Mandala imprint of Unwin Hyman books, now owned by HarperCollins; by happy coincidence the publishers of this book! I was in heaven. My job was to work on books that explored everything that fascinated me: new age, astrology and spirituality. I met a bunch of fascinating authors, attended countless workshops, seminars and lectures and learned a great deal. I nearly didn't get the job, though, but for yet another heaven-sent coincidence.

When I left university I applied for numerous jobs and didn't get any of them. Each rejection set me back a great deal. I loved books and knew I wanted to work in the publishing industry but doors didn't seem to be opening. I'd clam up in interviews; my lack of self-confidence was really working against me. I also wasn't terribly good at details and failed basic editing assessments. It makes me laugh now as I often spend days speed typing but back then I was truly hopeless; even being asked to type up a basic letter freaked me out.

One Monday afternoon I was travelling home from London after yet another unsuccessful interview. There were big delays on the railways – nothing much has changed, has it! Anyway, my train was cancelled and there wouldn't be another one for an hour. I wandered around Waterloo station for a while feeling a bit lost. Back in those days stations weren't such great places to hang out, but I did find a cold bench to sit on.

I was soon joined by a couple of guys with some delicious-smelling fish and chips. I shuffled to the end of the bench, trying to ignore my rumbling stomach, and started reading my newspaper. The guys were quite noisy talkers and I couldn't help but overhear that they were students at the London College of Publishing and Printing. Like me, it seemed they were in the process of applying for jobs in the publishing industry. One of them was excited about an interview his tutor had fixed him up for next week at Unwin Hyman books. He said the only drawback was that he had to pretend he was into all that psychic stuff but he'd read a few books in the next few days to get clued up. My ears pricked up and I took mental note. I phoned the publisher the next day and asked for application forms. Needless to say I got the job because I didn't need to pretend I was into that 'psychic stuff'.

If my train hadn't been delayed that day I might never have got the job that was perfect for me. Remember, this was back in the eighties and books about the psychic world and jobs working with them were far rarer than they are today. If I'd got any of the other jobs I applied for in publishing it wouldn't have worked out because the subject matter would not have engrossed me. At the time I took all these coincidences for granted but looking back, I truly feel that I was being guided in the right direction.

It was when I was working as an editorial assistant that I discovered what I really wanted to do with my life. I wanted to write the kind of books I was working on. I loved writing the blurbs on the backs of the books and the authors were always so pleased with what I had done. I enrolled on an evening course in writing and journalism and started to get a steady trickle of small jobs for mind body spirit and healthy living magazines.

Several twists and turns of fate later I ended up living in Dallas, Texas. I wasn't writing books yet but I had got the process started by working in journalism. I was also very happily married by then with a baby boy complicating my life in a delicious way.

It was while I was living and working in Dallas that a psychic doorway opened – I heard my mother actually speak to me in my dreams. As anyone who has lost a loved one knows, it's one thing helping other people cope with the loss of a loved one but a whole new ball game when that person is you. I'm 43 years old now. I've had my heart and my bones broken and lost close friends, but nothing will ever compare to the pain I felt when my mother died after a year-long battle with colon cancer that spread to her liver.

I was 25 when she died and the pain was deep, wrenching and unbearable. I would have given anything for a sign from her that she was still with me, watching over me, but nothing came. I cursed my lack of ability to see, hear or touch her or make contact in any way. I felt like a failure. My brother tried to ease my suffering by telling me he sensed her presence constantly around us both but that didn't help much. Why didn't she make contact with me? Why wouldn't the angels speak to me?

I got very disillusioned. I questioned my assumptions about the afterlife. I challenged my mum to prove to me that she hadn't gone but all I got was silence. What I didn't realize in the years that followed was that she was sending me gifts from the afterlife all the time but I wasn't ready to see them. My radar was tuned too low and I questioned what I should have instinctively known. My mother was constantly whispering to me. I just wasn't listening.

For several years after she died I would for no apparent reason tear through my house, desperately trying to find a photograph of her. I was terrified that I had forgotten what she looked like. I needed to remember. Then at night she would visit my dreams. She seemed so real. She walked, talked and laughed. She didn't speak to me directly but she had all the endearing mannerisms I loved. She also appeared healthy, happy and whole. The last few weeks of her life as she battled cancer she had lost her glow, but in my dreams she was vibrant again.

But dreams weren't enough for me! I wanted my mother to talk to me, to appear to me, to give me advice like she always used to. I wanted her to show me there was an afterlife. I didn't recognize their impact on my life at the time but the dreams I had of my mother were a great gift from the afterlife. They were so regular and frequent that they did unconsciously give me the strength I needed to keep moving forward with my life. Dreams, along with coincidences, are perhaps the easiest ways for spirits to communicate with those of us still in the physical world. They are also the form of communication least likely to alarm or cause fear for the dreamer. With my nervous disposition, that's probably why my mother chose dreams as her first way to keep in touch with me.

It wasn't until eight years after she had died, when I'd done some growing up and calming down, that my mother actually made contact with me in a night vision. It wasn't like the dreams I'd had of her before when she didn't seem to be aware of me. In this dream I wasn't witnessing her, she was aware of me. She was interacting with me. She was speaking to me. The full story is in the introduction but, to briefly recap, she told me to take the right path and because I followed her advice the following day my life was saved. This dream unlocked a psychic door and a few months later that door was flung wide open when I heard the voice of my mother at the birth of my daughter. This time she wasn't speaking to me in dreams, she was speaking to me when I was fully conscious. I couldn't see her but I could feel her and hear her so clearly it was as if she was standing next to me.

'You are making things worse for yourself than they need to be,' I heard my mother say to me when I was in labour. 'Don't let your fear of the unknown give you even greater pain. You can do this. I know you can.'

In the first few days of my daughter's life my mother's words went around and around in my head. I was being given a clear wake-up call from the afterlife. It suddenly became clear to me that gifts from the afterlife had been showered on me in the past through dreams, hunches and coincidences, but I hadn't been able to recognize them for what they were.

All these years that I had thought I wasn't psychic I had been psychic all along – I just hadn't realized or accepted it. And the reason why I had not accepted it was fear. I was frightened of not fitting in. I was frightened of being called weird. I was frightened of not living up to my mother. I was frightened of what my dreams, my sudden hunches and my feelings would tell me about myself and others. I was frightened of my own power. Until I recognized that my fear was holding me back I couldn't understand or interpret these feelings. I needed to relax. I needed to stop trying so darn hard. I needed to listen to my intuition, rather than try to explain it.

In the past I'd convinced myself that the reason people, even those I didn't know very well, would often open up to me was because I looked friendly and non-threatening. But now I could see clearly that I have the natural gift of empathy. I just lacked confidence in it. Empathy is the first step to psychic awareness. It's the ability to imagine what things look or feel like for some-one else. Have you ever imagined what it would be like to be someone else? Have you ever sensed the feelings of joy, loss, sadness or excitement before the person actually experiencing them tells you about them? This is empa-thy at work.

Empathy is a gift everyone – yes everyone – has. Even scientists agree that we are all born mind readers. Think about it. Whether we know it or not, without the ability to empathize with the thoughts and feelings of others, we couldn't handle the simplest social situations – or achieve true intimacy with others. To unlock the hidden potential of empathy, however, you need to trust it. My lack of self-belief had been the barrier or block to my psychic development all these years. Like everyone, I had had the gift all along. I just needed to believe in it and go with it.

I often wonder how many other people there are out there, like me, who want to see and hear an angel so desperately that they strain to do so. But any time people try too hard they are coming from a place of fear. It could be an anxious thought that maybe you're doing something wrong or that the angels can't hear you, or some other ego-based concern. The ego is entirely fear-based and until you can get beyond it, psychic development is blocked.

After that breakthrough of awareness in the months and years following my daughter's birth everything changed for me, for the better. I stopped feeling frightened of my experiences. I started to relax and embrace them instead. And as soon as I stopped doubting my abilities and trying too hard to connect with angels things started to fall into place in my life. I didn't have to struggle anymore. I didn't have to chase the writing career that I had longed for; it found me. I didn't have to chase angels; they found me.

By then I had moved back to the UK and my dream of transitioning from journalism to writing books was realized. I listened to my inner voice, put myself forward for opportunities and came into contact with some remarkable people. My first books were about health, diet and wellbeing, and when a couple of these went on to become bestsellers I was finally in a position to concentrate on what I really wanted to work on: books about the world of spirit.

In the ten or so years I've been writing full time I've had the privilege to write for inspirational mediums such as Tony Stockwell and Derek Acorah and celebrity ghost hunter Yvette Fielding. I've written a series of books for teenagers on how to develop their psychic powers as well as several books and numerous features on developing and working with your sixth sense. As a result, my postbag and email have swelled over the years with incredible stories from people of all ages and from all over the world, detailing their psychic adventures and angel encounters. I've written a heavyweight *Encyclopaedia on the Psychic World*, followed by an *Encyclopaedia of 20,000 Dreams* – which went on to become an international bestseller. Then I had the most remarkable gift from the angels. I was asked to write this book. What a gift! What an honour!

Most people can't believe that I'm not a celebrity but I've somehow had book after book published. They say I must be lucky to be writing about what I love. I have great delight in telling them that my life hasn't been easy. I grew up in poverty and left school at 16 with no qualifications. The reason for my success now is that

I finally learned to listen to the angels in my life and hear what they are saying to me. There isn't a day that goes by that I don't feel deeply grateful for their watchful guidance.

This isn't to say I don't have problems or setbacks any more. I have my fair share of disappointments and rejections and flickers of self-doubt like everyone else. There are times when I encounter more questions than answers. There are times when I look at the injustice and violence in the world and bang my keyboard, head and heart in pain and frustration. But what has changed is that I've learned to get a handle on my fear. I'm willing to learn and grow from setbacks and criticism, not feel destroyed by them. I'm willing to see the positive in everyone and everything, including myself. I'm willing to believe in the impossible because I know from my own experiences that nothing in life is ever ordinary. I'm willing to accept that sometimes bad things happen to good people for reasons I can never fully understand. I'm willing to trust and let the voice of my guardian angel help me fly through this life and the next.

There have been other astonishing events in my life, but there isn't time for that here. I just hope that reading about some of my experiences has given you a better idea of where I'm coming from before I open up my case files for you. I hope that as you read on you will be as moved as I was by some of the true stories that I've gathered over the years and reported for you in this book.

There's just one more thing before you move on: I'd like to encourage you to share your own angel experiences with other people. Remember, every angelic encounter is unique. Angels appear in different ways to each person so if you aren't sure if an angel is calling your name, listen to your heart; it will know the answer.

Don't be afraid to share. Fear and low self-esteem are, remember, natural predators of the angels. They limit the volume and clarity of the messages your heavenly guardians want to send you. So, instead of doubting your guardian angel, try looking at how you already have received messages from heaven and how much goodness, humour and happiness there already is in your life as a result. It really is much easier than you think. And the more we all open our hearts to one another the closer to earth our angels will fly, reminding us that we are never alone.

CHAPTER 2

Miraculous Messages from Beyond

The voice of an angel can unlock hidden feelings.
If you have trouble hearing with your ears, try
listening with your heart.

Anon

Although you may not actually 'see' an angel in the physical sense, they are never far away. Have you ever had a sudden or unexplainable change of heart and wondered, 'Where did that come from? That's the last thing I thought I would do or agree to'? That's the work of your angels guiding you in the direction you need to go. Have you ever felt completely wretched, feeling that a situation is hopeless and impossible to resolve and then suddenly out of nowhere everything changes? You are filled with hope and optimism. It's your angels at work again.

Have you ever felt forgotten and alone and then a soft breeze on your hand or a gentle touch on your cheek revitalizes you? That's the touch of an angel to let you know you are not alone. And have you ever thought someone was watching you – that intense feeling that someone is behind you? Yet you turn around and there is no one there? There is someone there after all – an angel!

In recent years there have been many occasions when I have been absolutely convinced someone was standing behind me or watching me. The hairs on the back of my neck have even stood on end. Then when I turned around I could see no one there. The sensation most typically occurs when I am writing alone in my office but it has also happened when I've been in a room with other people or out in the street. There is no specific prompt or trigger but it is more likely to happen if I'm feeling stressed or anxious. When I work on my computer on a book or a feature with a pressing dead-line for far longer than I should do the sensation gently reminds me that it is time to stop, take a break, refresh my eyes and smell the flowers.

I never feel alarmed or threatened by these 'he's behind you' experiences, as I like to call them; quite the opposite. I feel peaceful and light-hearted because I know my guardian angel is watching over me. But I'm well aware that other people who also have this experience on a regular basis – and it is far more common than you realize – may think they are being overanxious, nervous, paranoid, even.

The best thing to do if you get this sensation is to stay calm and to breathe deeply. Double check that no one is actually standing behind you or that you aren't in any kind of danger. One night when I was walking down a back street in London with my brother he experienced this sensation and we both ran as fast as we could, narrowly escaping a mugging! If the coast is clear – as it almost always is, especially when you are alone – celebrate the closeness of your guardian angel. Thank your angel for watching over you and reminding you of their comforting presence. Use the sensation to open your heart and your mind and ask for guidance and inspiration.

You may have heard stories of people who have seen and even spoken to angels – and you'll find incredible stories like that later in the book – but you've probably heard less about the touch, scent, whisper, laugh, kiss and other gentle signs that angels use to alert us to their presence or to protect us from harm. But all these miraculous things are possible, as these true stories show. The thread joining everything here is that none of the people actually saw an angel complete with bright lights, feathered wings and halo. Yet they remain convinced that angels dipped into their lives and somehow made them stronger, happier and greater than they believed themselves to be.

Angel's Kiss

There is a story that explains why we all have a little groove above our mouth and below our nose, called the philtrum. According to the story this little groove is called an Angel's kiss: on the day we are born we already know all about the angelic world, but our guardian angel puts a finger there to help us forget, so that we don't spend our lives full of regret and longing to return.

This story reminds us that angels are healers, protectors and bearers of wisdom, but most of all they are our friends. They laugh with us and they cry with us. They know us better then we know ourselves and even though we can't always see or hear them, as Nicola's story shows, they always have our best interests at heart.

Invisible Kisses

My mother always told me that she didn't want me to see her body after she had died. She wanted me to remember her alive and vibrant so when the doctor asked if I wanted to say one last goodbye I said no.

A day before the funeral my aunt and uncle asked the same question and once again I said no. They pressured me, saying that even though she had lost a lot of weight she looked peaceful, but I remembered what my mum had told me. I was pressured again by my husband who told me that seeing my mum would be a healing process, but I had made my mind up. Everyone said I would regret my decision one day.

About an hour before the funeral I went to my bedroom to gather my thoughts. Tears welled up in my eyes. I thought of my mother lying cold and motionless in her coffin. Perhaps I should have given her one last kiss? Perhaps everyone was right and I needed the closure?

At that moment I felt a refreshing breeze on my face. The breeze was so strong it wiped some of my tears away. My bedroom door was closed and there were no windows open. I knew it was my mother.

During the funeral I focused on the happy times mum and I had shared and as I said my last goodbyes I felt invisible lips kiss my cheeks on both sides. I closed my eyes and saw an image of my mum smiling and dancing, just as she wanted me to remember her. I knew then that I had made the right decision. From then on, whenever I thought of her she would always be dancing and smiling by my side.

There are many ways for our loved ones to come to us, to affirm that they are still living in spirit. Invisible kisses and puffs of air are often reported, as are scents. The strong smell of chocolate is a common theme. Flower scents are also frequently reported, in particular strong-smelling ones like gardenias, roses and lavender. This is Margaret's moving story.

Winter Roses

Eric was my soulmate and it was hard for me to contemplate life without him. We had been married for 25 years. We met when we were both 18. I can remember the first time I saw him. We were both invited to a mutual friend's party. I was incredibly shy but this handsome, confident guy just came over and introduced himself. He made me laugh and we talked all evening. When it was time to leave he offered to walk me home.

That walk home was magical. It was snowing but I felt warm inside. Eric told me that the thing he hated most about winter was that the rose-growing season was over. He loved the smell of roses in summer. I can't explain why but it was at that exact moment that I knew I was in love with him. Eight years later we were married. When we moved into our first home one of the first things we did was plant dozens of rose bushes in our garden.

I can honestly say we had a wonderful marriage; sure, we had our disagreements but the love between us was so strong it could conquer anything. We weren't blessed with children but we were blessed with each other. Losing him after a two-year battle with prostate cancer felt like the end of the world for me. I stopped eating. I stopped going out. I wanted to die. I made a few fragile attempts to step back into life but I missed my Eric so badly I thought I would never be able to go on.

Then one night in the middle of winter I woke up and there was a heavy scent of roses in the air. I got up and went into the garden. There was thick snow covering the rose bushes and the ground was frozen. The scent was definitely coming from inside the house even though there were no fresh or dried flowers inside. As I went from room to room the scent seemed to grow stronger. It's hard to describe, but I knew Eric was there with me using the scent of roses in winter to take me back to the moment I fell in love with him. He was trying to comfort me. He was sending me a message that I was still living and my life needed to go on. I started to cry because I knew that he wanted me to let go. As I made a silent promise to him to move on the scent vanished.

Although I shall miss Eric deeply until the day I die, the scent of roses that night gave me the strength I needed. It was his way of letting me know that he is watching over me. He had always said if there was a way to reach me after death he would; so he was just keeping his promise.

Stories of clocks stopping, lights flickering, alarms bleeping and music suddenly playing are other surprisingly typical ways for loved ones to let us know they haven't left us. George shares his remarkable experience.

Wake Up and Smell the Coffee

My sadness was drowning me. I felt that my life was useless. My wife had died suddenly. I could not accept that she had gone. Why did she have to go now when we had retired early to enjoy life?

A week after my wife died our dog, Poppy, stopped eating. She got so weak I had to have her put to sleep. Two losses within a month! I lost a stone. I wasn't eating. Food didn't interest me. Life didn't interest me.

My brother and sister-in-law called round every day to invite me for coffee or to go shopping. Friends phoned and letters and cards dropped through the letterbox but wherever I went it was always the same – I was alone. A year passed like this and then the 'signs' started.

One night my sister came for dinner. She suggested visiting the dogs' home the following day to choose a new dog. She told me that taking care of the dog and getting lots of fresh air walking it would do me the world of good. I told her in no uncertain terms that I wasn't ready for a dog. I wasn't ready for anything. I asked her to leave. No sooner had she shut the door behind her than the light bulb blew in the hall. I didn't think anything of it but then I went into the kitchen and another light bulb blew. I looked at my watch. It was just after 7 pm so I decided to get some new bulbs in the morning.

I slumped on the sofa to while away the hours watching television. I must have nodded off briefly because I woke with a start. The TV wasn't on. I tried fiddling with it but it wouldn't work. Then all of a sudden I heard a noise coming from upstairs. I rushed up into my bedroom and saw that my wife's jewellery box was open. The little ballerina inside was twirling around to its Swan Lake tune. I had given it to my wife as a first anniversary present. It had stopped playing many years ago, although my wife had tried it many times.

I went back downstairs and as I stood in the hall, I felt a cool breeze go by me. Then I was hit by the strong aroma of coffee I used to smell every morning when my wife was up making breakfast and toast. I knew then that my wife had come to help me. On the floor was the note my sister had left with the phone number of the dogs' home. My wife wanted me to love something again.

Elated, I rang my sister saying I had changed my mind and I did think a dog was a good idea. She was delighted but sounded a little disorientated. I asked her what was wrong and she asked me if I knew what time it was. I glanced at the clock on my mantelpiece and it said 7 pm. My sister told me that my clocks must be wrong because it was actually 11 pm. I looked at my wrist watch and it also said 7 pm, exactly the time my sister left that evening.

The next morning I did go to the dogs' home and I chose a beautiful little puppy. Taking care of and training a new dog was exactly the tonic I needed. I know my wife is still with me, especially in the mornings when I wake up and smell the aroma of coffee coming from the kitchen downstairs, even though I actually drink tea instead of coffee. My wife was the coffee pot every morning, not me. My new dog recognizes the smell. He will often get up on all fours and begin sniffing around in the kitchen, raising his head up and sniffing the air. I'm so glad he can smell it too.

I'm aware that so far the stories in this chapter have been rather serious but it is important to point out that angels have a whimsical sense of humour. I often feel them smiling or laughing with me – especially when daft things happen, like the time I bought a brand new trendy leather jacket and trousers to impress an editor I was going to work with. When I turned up at her office the doorman told me that I should leave my delivery around the back! Angels don't always take themselves seriously and sometimes they try to encourage us to do the same by communicating their love through humour, as Sarah's delightful story shows.

The Final Chapter

My family is extremely close. Every year since we were children we gather together for Christmas and it is always a time for love, laugher and celebration. The same people, the same delicious food, the same jokes! It may seem boring to some people but it is comfortable and cosy for me.

Year after year we share wonderful moments and memories but in the last few years I noticed not just my own advancing age but my father's slower pace as well. Last year, after dragging the Christmas tree up a flight of stairs, his eyes bright with anticipation, he fell and broke his hip. His routine hip surgery went well but the medical team noticed a problem with his blood count and ordered further testing. The tests revealed that dad had liver cancer.

And so that Christmas instead of laughing over our mince pies we were sitting anxiously in a hospital waiting room. About three months and two different hospitals later dad was finally allowed to go home. We made the day really special. We bought him all his favourite food, music and books and he spent the next few weeks reading, relaxing and chatting with us all.

Although we knew it was coming, the morning my mum woke to find that he had died in the night was still a shock. Feeling numb with grief I helped plan the funeral. Our family was incomplete now and I wondered if we would ever laugh again. Dad had always been such a practical joker and his lively, curious mind meant that conversations were never boring. I was 45 years old and I had never spent Christmas without my dad – I couldn't imagine it without him now. There were too many things that would not be the same.

My grief was nothing compared to my mother's loss and loneliness. After a long and happy marriage it was disorientating for her to be alone in the world without the sound of his voice, without the comfort of knowing he was there in the next room reading his books, waiting for her to join him.

I've always been an early riser, like my mother, and now with my dad gone I was up even earlier than normal. I didn't want mum to go without the sound of someone's voice for too long, alone with her thoughts and memories. One morning her voice sounded different. It was full of surprise and wonder instead of the sadness I had grown used to.

'I have a mystery in my hands,' she said, holding a book out towards me. She then went on to say that when she had got up that morning she found a copy of *The Da Vinci Code* open on the floor. 'How did it get there?' she asked me. I didn't have a clue. My mum was a very tidy person. She didn't read in bed and books would always be put away downstairs in the bookcase.

Later that day I shared the story with my husband, Robert, and he stared at me with his mouth open. 'That is incredible. Don't any of you remember what your mum said about the last conversation she had before she went to bed the night your dad died? When she helped him into bed he asked her if he could finish reading the final chapters of *The Da Vinci Code* because he wanted to know what the ending was. And she said it was too late but when he woke in the morning she would make him a cup of tea and read him the final chapters herself.'

Listening to this, my eyes started to sting as I pictured in my head my mother kissing my dad for the last time. So it was dad who had left the book open on the floor that morning. The open book was his light-hearted way of saying that there is another life after this one. He was just reading his final chapters in another room and waiting for us to join him.

Another story – this time from a man called Mark – and another angel with a sense of humour.

Divine Comedy

I was in a state of complete panic when I lost my mobile. Today was a crucial make or break day for me at work. My mobile had all my business contact numbers and without it my day would be chaos. I started to beg for help from on high. I wondered if angels really existed. If they did, would they really bother helping me find such an everyday item?

I remembered that I had stopped in a coffee bar that morning. It seemed logical to go back there to see if some kind soul had handed my mobile in. On entering I saw that the place was packed and the staff rushed off their feet. I was about to leave when a barista clearing up a table asked me if I was looking for something. I told her I may have lost my mobile and was delighted when she said that she had found one and put it safe behind the counter. When she came back with my mobile in her hand I wanted to thank her personally, so I looked at her name card. Her name was Angelina. I hadn't seen her at the coffee bar before and I haven't seen her since.

One of the things I have always found so hard to accept about spiritual retreats and gatherings is that everyone looks so serious and earnest. I remember once going to a summer solstice celebration. When I got there almost everybody was wearing black and the 'celebrations' consisted of mournful music playing in the background, lectures about the looming threat of global warming and if you didn't fancy that you could sign up for an impossibly difficult yoga session with a teacher who had had a sense of humour bypass. The only refreshment on offer was watered-down orange juice and rich tea biscuits. I'm not joking! Thankfully, stories like the ones above prove that not only do angels have a sense of humour, they also love to hear the sound of our laughter. They don't take themselves too seriously and neither should we.

As well as lightening our hearts with laughter and offering gentle messages of comfort, guidance and inspiration to those willing to listen with an open heart and an open mind, angels can intervene more directly in our lives through the healing power of touch. What Kate experienced offers powerful testimony that angels don't always conform to the stereotypical 'mystical' image, complete with wings and white gowns. They can also be extremely practical, direct and hands on.

Unseen Hands

On many occasions in my life I have felt that angels are near, but on one occasion I am certain that one actually touched me – or rather hit me.

I was 15 at the time and boys rather than angels were on my mind. My mum was very health conscious and always nagging me to eat my fruit and vegetables. She used to put a bowl of apples in my bedroom in the hope I'd snack on them rather than on junk food.

One night my brother was staying overnight with a friend and my mum went to bed early. It was a situation I loved – staying up late in my room with the door shut, listening to music and dreaming about a boy I fancied with no one to bother me or send me on errands or tell me to tidy my room. I had a chilled-out night and at about midnight I decided to go to bed. I got changed into my night clothes. I felt a bit peckish and for once was grateful to my mum for leaving a bowl of fruit in my room.

I grabbed an apple, took four or five very big bites, turned out the light and flopped into bed lying face down.

It felt as if my lungs were bursting and I couldn't get any air. I tried to call mum but could only gasp. A piece of apple was stuck in my throat. I was choking to death. Suddenly I heard the door open. I heard no footsteps but someone whacked my back once. The blow was hard but I spat out the piece of apple and air instantly filled my lungs. I rolled over expecting to see my brother or my mother. There was no one in my room. The house was as quiet as it had been all night.

Still shaking, I stumbled into my mum's bedroom and woke her up. She was astonished and we both searched the house. My mum asked me if I had been dreaming but I told her I most certainly had not. I had felt this huge hand on me. My mum asked me to turn around and she gasped and told me to have a look over my shoulder in the mirror. Although it was beginning to fade there was a definite mark on my back but it wasn't the mark of a normal hand it was the mark of something much bigger.

I can recall the events of that night as if they happened yesterday. The mark has faded but my memory of it hasn't. I can't tell you how comforting it is for me to know that an angel saved me from choking that night.

Remember the smell theme mentioned previously, when a grieving widow was comforted and encouraged by the smell of winter roses? We're returning to it here. George, a retired entrepreneur, tells this enchanting tale.

Heaven Scent

About ten years ago I was, in the eyes of the world, extremely successful. I ran my own business and it was thriving. I lived in a large house in a leafy suburb and had a holiday home in Spain. I had a lovely wife and three beautiful grown-up children thriving in their jobs or at university. I had a close circle of friends and my health was good. My cup was full; but looking back I wasn't nearly as fulfilled as I thought I was.

Ever since my children left home I had kind of lost my way. Instead of slowing down to deal with my feelings of loss and fear of getting old I speeded up. I expanded my business and invested in several properties abroad. I splashed out on a ridiculously expensive Porsche I didn't really need.

One Sunday afternoon my wife and I were invited to an afternoon gathering by Alan, one of my oldest friends. Alan had been a great help me to in the early days of my business, offering to lend me money when no one else would and I was forever in his debt. When we arrived at the party everyone present was well dressed and eloquent but there was one person completely out of place. Sitting hunched and dishevelled in a distant corner with a confused expression on his face was a middle-aged man. His clothes looked like they had come from a charity shop. I had never met him before and when I asked Alan who he was I was immediately introduced to 'Thomas'. Reluctantly, I held out my hand and Thomas grabbed it, grinning enthusiastically and revealing a set of yellow teeth.

It was then that this smell hit me. This guy smelled strongly of lavender soap. I remember thinking how strange it was for someone so untidy to smell so good. I scanned the room for Alan to rescue me but he was mingling with other members of the group and had his back turned to me. I stayed for a few moments with Thomas, and talked about the weather I think, before pretending I needed to go to the rest room.

It was a lazy Sunday afternoon so we stayed at the gathering, enjoying the tonic of good conversation and good food. As people were starting to drift home Alan took me aside and asked me to if I could do him a big favour. He told me that he had joined a volunteer programme and was giving Thomas a ride every day from his doctor back to his care home. He was going on holiday for ten days the following week and needed someone to take Thomas instead while he was away.

I quickly glanced at Thomas nodding off in the same corner that I had left him and said to Alan, 'Look mate,

I really don't think I'm the person you should be asking. I'm rushed off my feet at the moment with work and the new properties. I just don't think I've got the time.' Alan looked disappointed so I tried to make a joke of it. 'Have pity, mate. I've just bought a brand new Porsche. It's my pride and joy. No offence, but this guy would cramp my style.'

I tried to walk away but Alan wouldn't have any of it. He grabbed my arm, looked me directly in the eye and told me that it really wasn't much to ask and besides I owed him. I was shocked. This was the first time Alan had ever tried to use emotional blackmail. I wasn't having it. I didn't want anything to do with this uncouth Thomas guy. For the first time ever, Alan and I parted company that evening with a stilted handshake and pursed lips.

The next day as I was driving in my brand new Porsche, I was suddenly aware of a strong smell of lavender in my car. It reminded me of Thomas. I rolled down my windows thinking it must have come from outside.

The next day I gave my wife a lift in the Porsche and the lavender smell was as strong as ever. I asked my wife if she could smell it but she didn't know what I was talking about. I didn't know what was causing it. For the next few days, every time I drove the lavender smell would accompany me. Sometimes I thought it wouldn't arrive but within ten minutes of driving I felt like I was in a flower shop.

The Sunday after the party I got a phone call from Alan. He begged me to collect Thomas just this one time from the doctor because his wife was down with flu and he needed to be there for her. He said he had tried everyone else before calling me but they were either on vacation or out shopping and I was his last hope. I surprised myself by agreeing. I drove to the doctors and picked up Thomas, feeling more than a little ticked off that I was doing something I really didn't want to.

Thomas was waiting outside the surgery. He said, 'Thank you,' as he got into the car and shifted clumsily in his seat. I glanced at him nervously in my rearview mirror throughout the journey. He was watching the passing scenery with curiosity and excitement; just like my children used to when they were younger. He said nothing as I drove him to his care home, except, 'Thank you again,' as he was leaving. I watched him hobble into the centre and then drove slowly home. It was only when I was close to home that I realized that the lavender smell had mysteriously vanished from inside my car – or perhaps I had simply grown accustomed to it.

Alan called that evening to ask how everything went and to thank me. As the experience hadn't been as unpleasant or as inconvenient as I thought I found myself agreeing to be Thomas's taxi when Alan went on his holiday. And something amazing happened to me during those ten days. The time I thought I didn't have began to appear. I started to call Thomas by his name and he called me by mine. He was a man of few words but they were well-chosen words. On the last day we didn't go directly back to his care home. We stopped for a drink instead. I started to like this guy and although I saw people around him do a double take, it didn't matter to me any more. When I dropped him off for the last time that day and said he should expect Alan in the morning he turned around and said, 'Thanks mate. People never cease to surprise me. I had you down as a guy who only thought about himself and making money. I was wrong. That will teach me to judge others by the way they look.'

I couldn't believe Thomas was saying that. I was the one who had judged. I was the one who had got it wrong. When Alan returned from his holiday he was keen to hear how things had been going with Thomas. I told him everything had been fine; more than fine in fact, and I liked the guy. I was curious so I asked Alan to tell me a bit about Thomas and how he had ended up like this. Alan then told me that Thomas had once been a surgeon but had been forced to give up the job he loved after being hit by a cyclist five years earlier. The accident had left him with head, leg and back injuries from which he would never recover. He had no living relatives or family to take care of him. He now required daily medical monitoring and daily medication. He had seizures quite regularly, wobbled when he walked and couldn't drive.

Alan went on to tell me that he had witnessed one of the relentless seizures Thomas suffered from. During the seizure Thomas had lost control of his bodily functions and vomited on himself before losing consciousness. Paramedics had to be called to clean him up and get him back on his feet. Thomas felt deeply embarrassed by these incidents and concerned that other people might be bothered by unpleasant smells. He overcompensated by zealously washing and using bottles and bottles of lavender fabric conditioner on his clothes.

Driving in my car the next day, and the day after, without Thomas to pick up or drop off didn't seem so great. I had this fabulous car and this fabulous life but I missed helping Thomas. Somehow when I had been his taxi I hadn't felt so lost or directionless. I called Alan to ask if he would like to share the rides with Thomas. Alan happily agreed and for the next 18 months Thomas became a part of my daily routine and my life.

Although Thomas died over eight years ago, to this day his lavender scent is indelibly inscribed in my senses. I really met him against my will. If it were my choice I never would have allowed this helpless and unkempt looking man into my precious car and into my life. But Thomas taught me that angels can appear in many different forms and in circumstances you cannot expect or anticipate. I still don't know why my car smelled like him before he had even got into it. One thing I do know is that the scent

44

of Thomas taught a man suffering from a debilitating case of self-centredness and a critical case of hardness of heart to open his heart and his mind. That man was me.

George's story shows that angels can take us on journeys we didn't know we needed to go on and transform our lives in the most unexpected ways. In translation, the word 'angel' actually means messenger, and because the messages angels bring are always those of wisdom, guidance and inspiration they are also teachers.

Although Ruby did not recognize a distinctive scent as George did, she very clearly received a powerful and life-changing message from her angel. In her own words, she tells her story.

Lighting Up

Dad died of lung cancer when he was 62. Mum died of heart disease when she was 67. Like them I was a heavy smoker. When I was growing up, I used to think smoking was kind of glamorous and romantic. I associated it with laughter. When money was tight and they couldn't buy their cigarettes mum and dad would argue, but when they had them dad would light mum's cigarette.

I used to steal cigarettes from mum and dad; I don't think they ever realized. I would go into the bathroom and practise looking sexy as I exhaled. By the time I was 16

I was already smoking at least 20 cigarettes a day. Smoking stopped me eating too much and gaining weight. Whenever I felt nervous smoking gave me confidence.

The first thing I treated myself to when I got a job was a beautiful gold lighter with my initials inscribed on it. As the years passed and anti-smoking legislation began to take hold I enjoyed smoking more than ever. There was an instant sense of camaraderie among the smokers clustered in tight-knit groups outside buildings. I didn't have to try hard to make friends.

At the age of 33 I started to get a cough just like my mother. It was hard to run for the bus, up a flight of stairs or after my four-year-old son without struggling for air.

About a month after my dad died, I was sitting down, exhausted, in front of the TV and lighting up with my gold lighter. Wondering how I was going to take care of my son, handle my fulltime job as a PA and look after my mum who was now wheelchair-bound after a stroke, I had a sense that my father was sitting beside me. Unnerved I grabbed another cigarette and reached for my gold lighter. It had vanished. I tore the sofa apart but couldn't find it anywhere. It still hasn't turned up to this day.

Over the next five years mum's health rapidly deteriorated. The night before she died she begged me to stop smoking, and told me she didn't want me to end up like her. She didn't want her grandson to always be able to tell when I was coming because he could hear my hacking cough. As she lectured and pleaded all I could think of was going outside to light up. This is something I guess only a smoker can understand.

I never felt more alone after mum died. I missed her laugh, her love, even her cough. I smoked more than ever as somehow it made me feel closer to her. Then strange things started to happen. I would buy a pack of cigarettes and find them missing from my shopping bag when I came home. If I was outside matches would never light and lighters would never work. Or I'd start coughing so badly I couldn't keep a cigarette in my mouth long enough to smoke it. And then when I finally managed to light up something would distract me; the phone would ring and there would be no one there, pictures would fall off the wall or a light bulb would blow. It really freaked me out.

Then when I was sorting out mum's things I found a letter addressed to me. In it she begged me once again to quit smoking for my own sake and for the sake of her grandson. She didn't want my life to be cut short like hers had been. She wanted me to write a list of all the things I wanted to do. She wanted me to set a date to quit.

Mum's letter got to me. I circled a day to quit on my calendar and as I did I felt a bolt of energy go through my body. My parents were there with me, spurring me on. A day before the date I was in a panic. I had been a smoker for as long as I could remember. Cigarettes kick-started my day, kept boredom away, helped me feel confident, helped me think and helped me chill out. How could I give up? Cigarettes were my life. I remembered my mum's letter. I thought about all the things I wanted to do. I wanted to run the marathon. I wanted to learn the piano. I wanted to surf.

On the day I was to quit I woke up sweating. Then I closed my eyes and I saw my mum and dad hugging me and telling me they would give me strength. I wasn't alone. It was incredible. In that instant I knew I was going to do it. I felt calm and in control and surrounded by love. I wasn't doing this alone. My parents who had been through so much with me were with me now.

In the hours that followed I had my moments of weakness, especially when things weren't going well or my son was playing up. But every time I felt tempted to grab a cigarette a voice in my head, my mother's voice, asked me how a cigarette would help make things better.

With the help of mum and dad I got through the first and hardest day. After that, as the nicotine passed out of my bloodstream I felt it being replaced by a new sense of energy and fun. Before I quit I was smoking 50 cigarettes a day. I feel more alive now. I am tasting food for the first time. I can smell the flowers again. I feel young, like a child learning everything for the first time: how to drive without a cigarette, how to talk without a cigarette, how to see the world around me without a cigarette. It's like being finally freed from a cage. Being a non-smoker means breaking free. I used to be a slave to cigarettes and they controlled my life. Now, I enjoy fresh breath, more money, dating non-smokers, a cleaner home and no more stale smell in my car. I look forward to my new life and, best of all, my son will no longer have to breathe in second-hand smoke.

The only good thing that I got from all those years of smoking was this great feeling of victory I got when I finally quit. I couldn't have done it, though, without the love and guidance of mum and dad. I know they are still with me every step of the way. They are helping me live out my intended years instead of coughing myself to an early grave. Supported by their love, I am a non-smoker today and will be a non-smoker for the rest of my life. The three of us will make sure of that.

This is another story that shows how angels can be messengers and teachers. Samantha, a catering assistant, tells how her guardian angel lightened her life; quite literally.

Light Years Ahead

I was in complete denial. My clothes stopped fitting me – but I just put that down to shrinking in the wash. (Yes, I thought all of my trousers and skirts had shrunk – mad!) I was convinced I was still slim and could eat what I wanted when in fact my weight was creeping up and up. I had to buy clothes two sizes bigger but convinced myself it was the shop sizing, not me.

Thing was, because I had always been underweight, my friends and close family wouldn't mention it. Eventually, I was at a wedding and joked that I would borrow the bride's dress for my own wedding and a friend (who was a bit tipsy!) laughed and said I'd be at least two sizes too big for it.

Even this didn't wake my mind up. The weight continued to pile on. I put on five stone over two years. I was constantly tired and constantly hungry. I couldn't turn my life around. I was trapped in a cycle of food cravings and overeating.

Then a photograph changed my life. One afternoon as I was sorting out my album a recent picture of myself with a group of friends fell on the floor. I bent down to pick it up. As I did the photograph started to change. It started to age. I saw lines and wrinkles appear on my face. I saw myself getting older but what made the picture so disturbing weren't wrinkles, but my ballooning weight. I got heavier and heavier in the picture; so heavy I had to be wheeled around in a wheelchair by my friends. Then I heard a gentle voice saying, 'This is one possible future. You have the power to change it.' The voice didn't frighten me. Instead I felt calm, strong, prepared. I knew what I had to do. It was time for me to take control of my weight.

Since that day I haven't looked back. I signed up for a weight-loss class and within a year I got down to my target weight of ten stone. Today I continue to eat healthily and exercise daily. I could never go back to the way I was. I love being slim again. I love buying clothes that fit me snugly and I love feeling good about myself. Of course, there are times when I'm tempted to indulge but my guardian angel's gentle voice comes to me loud and clear. It reminds me that I am loved and that I deserve a healthy and happy future.

Many people can feel the guiding presence of angels in their lives but how many actually write to them? Chloe, a tennis instructor in her late twenties at the time, was sceptical but as her story clearly shows her angels were listening; all they needed was clear instruction from her.

The Perfect Man

I used to have terribly bad luck with men. I always ended up being dumped or paying for everything or being last on their list of priorities. One of my pupils was really into angels and mystical stuff. I've always believed in an afterlife and we soon became friends. She'd often ask me about my love life and I'd share my tales of woe over a cup of tea.

Then one day she told me that my problem was that I wasn't giving my guardian angel anything to work with. I asked her to explain. She told me to go home and write down a description of who my ideal man was. I shouldn't stint on the details. I should write down what he would look like, what his personality was like and what his profession was. I should then pray to my guardian angel to send a man who matched that description into my life.

I didn't take her seriously but that night as I was about to go to bed I decided to give it a try. I didn't have anything to lose. I wrote down my wish list. I realized as I was writing that I hadn't really thought that deeply about the qualities I wanted in a partner. It took me almost an hour to come up with my perfect man. I fell asleep that night feeling a bit ridiculous. With my bad luck I was more likely to see an angel than meet a man with all the qualities I wanted. A week later I met him. He was the first man I'd been out with who held doors open for me and made me feel a million dollars. He was perfect for me and we've been married for a perfect twelve years and counting.

This story is in fact remarkably similar to my own. I'd also had terrible luck with men. If I'd listened to my intuition I could have avoided the heartache because there were always moments early on in each relationship that didn't eventually work out when a voice inside me urged me to back out but I ignored it. If I'd listened I would have saved myself a whole lot of heartache. It was only when I started to have a clearer sense of what I actually wanted in a partner that my luck in love turned around and I finally met my soulmate.

Divine Downloads

Angels aren't shy about using modern technology. As well as computers and televisions, they often use telephones or mobiles to communicate. Typically, this happens when people ask for a sign, then the telephone rings and there is no one there and when they use ringback the caller is unidentified or the number does not exist. It is rarer to hear a voice at the end of the telephone line but that is exactly what happened to Camilla, as she explains.

When I was about nine, my grandma was still alive. The last few years of her life must have been terrible for her as she suffered from Alzheimer's. I remember when my parents took me to see her in the nursing home where she lived and she just seemed to be wasting away. I was really scared to see someone so frail but my parents wanted me to visit her before she died.

A week after this I was sitting in the kitchen doing my homework when mum's mobile phone rang. I called mum to answer it but she was busy upstairs and asked me to. I rummaged through her bag and took the call. It was grandma.

'Hello. It's grandma here. Don't worry. Everything will be all right. Tell your parents. Don't worry. Everything's going to be fine.'

So I hung up and told my mum what grandma had said but she didn't believe me because grandma was too ill to be using phones.

An hour later we received a call from my great aunt. She told us that my grandma had died about an hour ago. This freaked me out as this was exactly the time I had received my phone call.

I didn't remind my mum about the phone call I had had as I knew they wouldn't believe me. It's a secret that I've kept with me all this time and it is such a relief to finally share it now with other believers.

Angels can also make their presence felt online in the ether, as Louise's inspiring story shows.

After my twin sister died I was inconsolable. We did everything together and knew everything about each other – or so I thought.

One day, about six months after the funeral, I went online and the image of my sister, Mary, appeared on screen. There she was. It was her. I saw her sitting in her

54

bedroom typing furiously on her laptop. I was surprised as we were both outdoor types and I never thought she was that into computers.

Then the image suddenly vanished and a web address appeared on screen. I clicked on the link and discovered that my sister had been keeping a blog. I had no idea. In her blog she talked a lot about school, her friends, mum and dad and me. She talked about how much she loved me and wanted me to live my dreams. She also talked a lot about angels and how she always felt surrounded by them.

I understood then that all this was to help me know she was okay and still looking out for me. I never used to believe in angels but I do now. I know for sure that Mary isn't gone and that she is with me all the time. I know because I've seen her.

Although I haven't yet come across any angel texts, emails and instant messages in my writing and information, I am convinced it is only a matter of time before I do …

Then there is Laura's story. The touch of an angel was particularly dramatic for her and, as with so many dramatic experiences, it took place at a time of great personal crisis.

Invisible Ink

Many years ago when I was in my early twenties, I suffered a very deep and dark depression following the birth of my first child. I was a single parent and back then there wasn't as much help and information available about post-partum depression as there is now.

After several weeks of deep depression, I came to a breaking point. I simply couldn't take care of my son any more; the dark feelings were too overwhelming. One evening after dropping off my son at my mum's for the evening I thought about packing my bags and leaving the country. My parents would take much better care of him than I ever could and one day he would understand.

I went back to my flat and with tears streaming down my face I started to write goodbye letters. As I was writing I suddenly felt as if someone was guiding my hand. Instead of writing, 'I'm sorry but I can't do this any more,' the invisible hand guided my pen to write, 'Mummy, don't run, you need to see me walk.' At first I was afraid. I threw the pen to the floor and the paper in the bin and grabbed another sheet and another pen. The same thing happened. Invisible hands were forcing me to write, 'Mummy, don't run.' I hadn't been drinking. I didn't know what to think. The experience shocked me so much that I didn't feel depressed any more. I felt elated. Those words gave me hope.

The next morning, I awoke for the first time in months feeling refreshed and as if I could walk on air. I looked at my desk and the crumpled pieces of paper where I had been writing the night before. I unfolded them carefully but they were all blank. I knew that I hadn't been dreaming. Invisible hands had made me write. What I had experienced was real.

I phoned my mum and dad and told them I'd be picking up my son early and from that day on I have treasured every second with him. He's a teenager now and the joy he has brought into my life is indescribable. It's me trying to snatch precious moments of time with him now before he flies the nest. Although I can't explain what happened that weekend I feel in my heart than an angel was guiding my hand to heal my heart when I wanted so desperately to run away. There are angels all around us. I was touched by their healing hands and will never forget them.

Laura's story is truly special. In the majority of cases it is parents who have the awesome task of offering comfort and reassurance to their children but from the depth of his love, Laura's baby son was guided by angels to work a miracle and offer hope and comfort to his overwhelmed mum.

The Voice of Your Guardian Angel

One of the most powerful and highly effective ways for your guardian angel to communicate love and guidance to you is through the voice of your intuition.

Intuition means knowing something without being aware of how you know it. It is an insight that seems to come from nowhere, a sudden knowledge without logical or rational explanation. It can come through a still, silent voice from within. Or it can be a feeling that you need to take it easy or run fast. It can be soft and gentle or it can be very strong.

There is growing evidence that we are all intuitive to some degree. This is exciting because it means that if we learn to listen we can all hear or tune into the voices of our guardian angels.

Split-second intuition can protect us from harm by telling us to run, hide, fight, look up or duck, and so on. If, however, there is no immediate threat, intuition is more likely to come to us when we are in a relaxed state of mind. Intuition can't be switched on and off and any attempt to do so or to work logically with it would be futile. Sometimes a walk, a good night's sleep, fun times with loved ones and simple feelings of awe and gratitude for what is good in our life are all that is needed for us to hear the familiar voice of our intuition.

Intuition, or the voice of your guardian angel, may come clearly first thing in the morning or in a dream with layers of meaning for you to unravel. On the other hand, you may physically manifest a message from your intuition. For instance, I always get headaches when I'm overdoing it. Or things that have special significance to you, such as a piece of music or a favourite food or wise words you have heard or read may appear in your life at exactly the moment when you need to feel supported, giving you peace of mind and courage. Your intuition may also speak to you in sections – a little piece now, a little piece a few days later. It is only when you have all the pieces of the puzzle that everything starts to become clearer.

We all hear voices in our heads but how can you tell whether it is your guardian angel or your fear talking to you? It can be tough to tell the difference. I think back to some of my early dating disasters. In the dark and lonely years following my mother's death I lost my bearings and my normally good judgement of character. I went out with a couple of men who certainly weren't right for me and even ended up in an abusive relationship. In each case I can think back to the first moment I met my boyfriend and every time the same thing happened. For a split second as I was talking to them their face or their body would become angular and distorted. I'd screw up my eyes and then they were back to normal. I'd convince myself that I was crazy and that I couldn't afford to be choosy. I listened to the voice of my fear, not my intuition.

On the first date I had with my future husband, after spilling hot tea over him and talking complete rubbish as I often do when I am nervous, I left convinced that I'd never see him again. The only voice I could hear in my head was one that told me I had messed up big time. I convinced myself that he didn't like me. There was no way he would want a second date so I deliberately avoided him. Once again I listened to my fear and it was trying to sabotage my chances of happiness and success. Fortunately, my husband managed to track me down. We had a second date and a third and many more and have been married for 14 happy years.

The voices we hear in our minds can be confusing but there are ways to tell the difference. When you know something intuitively, you just quietly know it. The feeling is very different from the noisiness of fear with its explanations that clatter around in your head. Intuition is also a lot gentler than fear. If the thoughts in your mind are full of self-doubt, anxiety and judgement they are the voices of fear. Intuition tends to be warmer, gentler, kinder and non-judgemental.

If the voices in your head say you are a loser, you always quit, you can't do what it takes, you're stupid, then this certainly isn't your guardian angel speaking. It's your fear. Your guardian angel would never say things to make you feel distressed. Your angel might tell you that something doesn't feel right. Or that this isn't the right thing for you and it's time to move on and try a new direction or approach to find what works better for you. There may be no words at all, just a gut feeling that it is time for a change.

Later in this book you'll find numerous stories which feature the voice of someone's guardian angel speaking clearly to them. In these stories the voice is soft, gentle, encouraging and convincing. Sometimes, it will be more forceful, challenging and direct but this is only if your safety or the safety of someone else is at risk. Barbara's story, below, is no exception. Barbara wrote to me to tell me about a reassuring voice from beyond that has thrown open a door of intrigue, wonder and hope between this life and the next for her and her family.

The Voice That Called My Name

I'd been trying to get pregnant for five years so when I got pregnant with Mary you can imagine how blessed I felt. My joy turned to panic, though, when Mary was born premature and came into this world weighing just three pounds. Being so small Mary's organs were not developed and we knew that the first weeks of her life would be a struggle between life and death.

At seven days old Mary became very ill. The only way to save her was a major operation that could take the better part of a day. John and I clung to each other as the hours ticked away for what seemed like forever. Twelve or so hours later we both fell asleep, feeling drained.

'Mummy, wake up,' I heard a sweet little voice with a slight lisp say. 'Wake up mummy. I'm ready to see you now.'

The voice woke me up and I nudged John and told him what I had heard. He told me I was just dreaming. I settled back down. I didn't sleep. I just lay there feeling completely relaxed and confident that everything would be okay.

A few minutes later a doctor came into the waiting room and told us that Mary was doing fine.

To this day I am convinced that the voice I heard was Mary's. I am certain because Mary is now six years old and I hear that sweet little voice with that lovely lisp every day.

When the voice of an angel is heard the experience is always revitalising and transforming. Linda's life was never the same again after hearing an angel whisper in her ear.

Calm Came Over Me

I was never one of those people who know where they are going in life. I dropped out of school and just drifted from one dead-end job to another; one dead-end relationship to another. My mum had passed when I was a little girl and my dad raised me by himself. We were very close but fell out when my dad didn't want me to leave school.

My dad always wanted me to go to university and get a good job but I was more interested in hanging around with my mates. I wouldn't listen. One morning after breakfast we had a huge argument. I stormed upstairs, packed my bags and went to stay with my best friend for a few nights. I got a job at a clothing warehouse to pay my way. If only I'd known that dad had just a few more months to live – that was typical of him. He never wanted to burden me with his worries.

After my dad passed, I was totally overcome with depression, grief, anxiety – you name it, I had it. I cried all night, begging my dad to come back and help me. I hated that the last time we had really spoken we had argued. I felt guilty and lost. I could not imagine getting on with my life without him: getting married, having a child or living any kind of life. This went on week after week. I went to my dad's grave during my lunch breaks, where I sat and cried.

Normally it took me ages to get to sleep but one night as soon as my head hit the pillow, I fell into a trance. I couldn't move or open my eyes. I was aware of where I was, but I felt frozen. At that moment I knew my dad was in the room. I did not see him, I just felt his presence and then I felt the side of the bed go down as if he was sitting on it. I felt him lean against my cheek and I heard him whisper in my ear. I couldn't understand what he was saying but I felt an unfamiliar calm came over me. I drifted off to sleep and woke up the next morning determined to turn my life around.

For the first time I didn't cry on the way to work. I knew what I had to do. I handed in my notice and put in my applications for college. Then I visited dad's grave and sat there, still savouring a feeling of calmness. It was the most astonishing thing. I couldn't explain it exactly but I felt as if a weight had been taken off my shoulders.

Although I haven't felt his presence since, I know dad was there that night. He knew what I was going through and came to comfort me and give me some good advice. To this day my encounter with my dad gives me hope and strength. I'm a qualified secondary school English teacher now. I'm determined to make a difference and help other kids find a sense of meaning and purpose in life. I know I'm making my dad proud.

Angelic Calling Cards

Angels can reach into this world in many ways and as this chapter shows, many people whose lives have been touched by an angel haven't actually seen one. Sometimes a silent whisper in the night or a gentle breeze on the cheek is all that it takes. Each person will experience angels in their own unique way and in most cases these experiences are deeply private and personal. But sometimes angels manifest their presence in ways that anyone can see.

Common angelic calling cards that I have come across in my research include cloud formations (where people see angels or lost loved ones in the shape of clouds), flowers that last longer or change colour and white feathers that appear in the most unlikely places. Once, when I was discussing angels with one of my editors I mentioned that white feathers are a common angel sign. My editor wasn't convinced but at that very moment a colleague noticed a pure white feather float to the floor beside her. The word 'angel' is another common way for the angels to let us know they are with us. Sometimes if you ask for angelic help, you will hear the word 'angel' mentioned in a song on the radio or on television, or you will read it online or in a book or magazine, or someone will say the word to you in the most unlikely context.

And don't forget that an angel story can act as an angelic calling card itself. You can read it at just the right time when you need comfort, guidance or inspiration, or are not sure what to do next. It can speak to you. It can open your mind. It can open your heart; the place where angels live. I'm therefore going to end this chapter with an angel story from Stephen, a secondary school head-master with 30 years' teaching experience. It's yet another example of the pervasive connections loved ones share, but in this case it shows how the loving words of one person to another can also work miracles.

A student in my sixth form English class had a very obvious birthmark over much of his face. His self-esteem seemed secure. He related well with the other students and was well liked; extremely popular in fact. He seemed to be in no way self-conscious about his very large birthmark, which was obvious to everyone else.

One day I overheard a friend of his ask him directly why his birthmark didn't seem to bother him. The young man wasn't shocked or upset but smiled and said, 'When I was very young, my father started telling me that the birthmark was there for two reasons: one, it was where the angel kissed me; and two, the angel had done that so my father could always find me easily in a crowd.'

He then continued, 'My dad told me this so many times with so much love that as I grew up, I actually began to feel sorry for the other kids who weren't kissed by the angel like I was.'

Perhaps we can all be instruments of the extraordinary, using loving words and acts of kindness to help others feel as if they have been touched by an angel. This wonderful angel quote says it far better than I can.

> We are each of us angels with only one wing, but we can only fly by embracing one another.
>
> **Luciano de Crescenzo**

CHAPTER 3

An Answer to a Prayer

Angels are never too distant to hear you and if
you seek an angel with an open heart you will
always find one.

Anon

The true stories in this chapter are astounding instances of
people whose lives have been touched by the miracle of
answered prayers. Angels, of course, play a central role here.
They act as intermediaries, helping to unburden our confusion and taking our yearnings directly to a higher power.

Have you ever felt a surge of strength, comfort and
peace when someone tells you that you are in their
prayers? Even though no one is exactly sure how it
works there is real power in prayer. Scientific researchers
in hospitals have even shown that patients who were
prayed for have faster release times. So instead of asking
our spirit helpers to lend a hand as a last resort, why not
ask for help straight away?

Praying, of course, doesn't always bring the answers or results we hope for. Some painful experiences are important lessons for the soul and why terrible things happen to decent or innocent people is beyond our limited comprehension, but if we ask the angels for what is best for us, they will be at our side helping to ease our pain and helping us find the inner strength to pull through. And if we do this on behalf of others, this strengthens the power of the angels to offer them healing, courage and comfort. Talk to people who have experienced personal tragedy or survived disaster and more often than not you will find that the trauma has helped them focus on what really matters: the priceless gifts of health, of love and of life.

So start asking the angels for their help, support and guidance today. Speak to them with confidence, enthusiasm and trust. Don't ever feel unworthy in any way. Yes, there will always be people whose need is greater than your own, but angels exist to help, and being there for you doesn't stop them helping others.

Angels can assist us in any number of ways. Sometimes they will reply in the form of a dream or a person appearing in your life at exactly the right time or in meaningful words that seem to speak directly to you. As we saw previously, angels can also respond in the form of a still small voice from within that speaks with gentle certainty when all around you there is chaos. They can make their presence felt in sudden flashes of insight when you inexplicably understand or know something with absolute clarity. Never ignore those gut feelings or 'light-bulb' moments as they could transform or even save your life.

Whether it's a remarkable coincidence or an astonishing turnaround of events that takes your breath away – these things are the angels at work. It doesn't matter how, where or when you choose to ask for their help, all you need to do is open your heart and invite them in.

As Linda's story shows, angels hear not only our formal requests, but also heartfelt prayers we don't even realize we are saying.

The Good Samaritan

It's about 25 years ago now but I can remember her sunny expression as clearly as if I saw her yesterday.

I'd just had my second child, Lucy, via C section. There were complications from the surgery and I was in constant pain. My mum was a huge support during my recuperation. She helped run errands for me and take my first child, Jake who was nearly six at the time, to and from school as I couldn't drive.

One cold and rainy November morning Jake was busy rehearsing his lines because he was going to perform in his school play that afternoon. I hadn't told him yet if

I would be able to come and see him or not. With Lucy nursing round the clock I felt guilty that he wasn't getting the time and attention he deserved from me. He was only six and understandably not as thrilled as everyone else seemed to be at having a baby sister. So when my mother arrived to collect him for school I promised him that I would be at his play in the afternoon come what may. His face lit up with a huge grin. I couldn't hug him to wish him luck as my sutures still hurt, but we were closer that moment than we had been for weeks.

Although I still felt sore, nothing was going to stop me going to the school play. Mum arrived just before lunch to pick me and Lucy up and suggested we stop at a local takeaway first to grab a bite to eat.

We drove to the takeaway and parked the car. Although it was starting to rain I felt stiff and sore and got out of the car to have a stretch. Just as mum got out and closed her door I saw her stiffen. She told me that she had left the keys inside the car and all the doors were locked. Lucy was still inside. Neither of us had a spare key and neither of us were members of an auto club. We cursed our carelessness.

Our only option was to call the emergency services. Mum went into the takeaway to ask if she could use a tele-phone and I waited outside, leaning on the car. Thankfully Lucy was fast asleep and unaware of the drama unfolding around her. It was raining quite heavily now and I was starting to feel unwell. I wasn't only worried about Lucy, I kept seeing Jake's little face scanning the audience anxiously looking for him mum, and me not being there. 'Oh Heavens,' I thought to myself. 'I just wish I could get in my car with Lucy and drive to Jake's school. I can't let him down now.'

Just as mum disappeared into the takeaway to find a phone a white car pulled up next to mine. A woman in a pale yellow T-shirt and light blue jeans got out. I noticed her immediately; thinking how strange it was to be just wearing a T-shirt on such a cold day. She looked about 20 years old and was really blonde and very pretty. She asked me if anything was wrong. With some embarrassment I told her that we had locked ourselves out of the car and the key was still in the ignition. My baby was inside sleeping but I was worried she could wake at any moment.

Without another word the woman opened her car door and pulled out a metal tool. In one easy movement she inserted the tool into the car door and popped open the lock. I was so happy to be able to get back into the car that I didn't have time to wonder how she had managed to do this so effortlessly. 'Oh, bless you, bless you,' was all I could think of saying.

The woman just smiled and said 'Bless you too, Linda.' She then peered into the back seat of my car and blew Lucy a kiss before getting into her car and driving away.

Mum came out of the takeaway. She was crying and preparing to tell me that the phones were down. She couldn't believe her eyes when she saw me smiling inside the car. I then told her how this remarkable young lady had arrived out of nowhere, popped open the lock and left. She obviously hadn't stopped for a takeaway. It was as if she had stopped just to help open the car door.

Elated, we drove to the school and got to the play with five minutes to spare. Jake was amazing and I was one proud mum. Lucy slept peacefully in my arms and didn't make a sound the whole time. That was a miracle in itself.

Later, my mum told me that the tool the woman probably used might have been a specialist tool that is only used by police and locksmiths to unlatch car doors. It was very unusual for ordinary people, in particular a young woman in those days, to carry one. And all these years later I can still recall my silent prayer, 'Oh heavens. I feel so bad. I just wish I was at Jake's school.'

Who was this woman in the white car? Was she just one woman helping another woman in need? But as she didn't stop for a takeaway how did she know Linda needed help? And how is it that she had exactly the right tool for the job? Of course, you could chalk this up as a Good Samaritan story crossed with a heavy dose of good fortune that this clued-up woman arrived just after Linda's mumbled plea for help, with exactly the right piece of equipment to unlock her car. But then how did this woman know Linda's name?

When someone does something kind or helpful we often refer to them as angels. This is because angels have a strong desire to help and to heal and it's no surprise to me that many of the stories I have heard and collected over the years involve angels helping and healing through the power of prayer in times of illness. Susan's story features a visit to a shrine; angelic presence is often intense at shrines due to the steady stream of prayers.

Lighting a Candle

I really needed a holiday. I hadn't had one for three years. As well as being a single mum and looking after my three children, aged 10, 14 and 15 and working full time I had my 80 year old mother to worry about. Although she lived alone she needed a lot of help running errands, especially since her arthritis had got worse. A home help did call round to check up on her once or twice a week and neighbours were attentive, but I still thought I should be close at hand. My mother, of course, was having none of it and when she found out that a friend was offering to let us stay in a villa in Spain for two weeks free of charge she told me in no uncertain terms to go.

The first week or so of the holiday was incredible. The kids soaked up the sun and I soaked up the sheer pleasure of having nothing to do and nowhere to go. I called my mum twice a day to check that she was all right but on the day before we were due to fly back she didn't answer the phone. I panicked and phoned again and again but there was still no reply. I called her home help and felt even more panicked when she told me that earlier that day my mum had been coming home from the shops and had had a flat drop; in other words she had fallen flat on her face. The home help told me that she was a bit bruised but being well taken care of in hospital. When I did finally manage to speak to my mum she told me she was in a lot of pain and was finding it hard to rest. I told her we'd be back the following day.

The last day of our holiday was hard to enjoy as my thoughts kept returning to my mum. I was frantic with worry. At around 4 pm after a day out in the countryside we found ourselves passing a chapel built in gothic and renaissance style. Normally, I would have been excited to stop and look inside as I love history and architecture but this time I didn't want to go inside. My children, however, were keen to explore so I told them they could look around while I waited inside the car.

Fifteen or so minutes later my children came back to the car with cheeky smiles on their faces. I asked them if they had found it interesting and they nodded enthusiastically. My ten-year-old told me that they had all lit candles for grandma and asked the angels to help her. This touched me deeply – and calmed me down too.

The next day we arrived back home and I immediately went to visit my mother. When I saw her I noticed the bruise on her face but I was amazed to see that she was sitting up and reading. Her voice was also animated and lively. 'I don't believe it,' she said. 'Yesterday at teatime I was in so much pain I couldn't even open my eyes and now look at me. I've been up today as well and went for a walk without any pain. I haven't been able to do that all year. Isn't it amazing?'

In a state of shock I told my mum how her grandchildren had prayed for her and lit candles at the exact time that she felt so much better. We both shed a few tears, convinced that a healing angel was hovering over us both.

Mandy has communicated with angels all her life and believes that this saved her son's life. Here is her story. Perhaps you recall the gentle but firm hands mentioned in a couple of the stories in chapter one? They make another appearance here.

The Hand That Touched Our Hearts

My son was born twelve weeks premature. His heart was frail and as soon as he was born I couldn't touch or hold him. He was whisked away and put on life support and monitored around the clock by a team of specialists. They were incredibly supportive but no one can prepare you for the devastation and shock when you are told to prepare for the worst. My husband was in pieces too but spared me the daunting, heart-breaking task of calling our families to tell them to prepare for a funeral rather than a celebration. I asked him to ask everyone to pray for us and for our little son. This would give everyone something to focus on rather than the pain and loss.

I prayed with all my heart and soul for the angels to take me instead of my son. Just talking about that terrible time makes me want to cry; unless you've been there yourself it is hard to convey how vulnerable, angry, guilty, devastated and frightened you feel. Every time the doctor walked through the door I braced myself to hear the worst.

The first 48 hours passed in a blur. Time stood still. I didn't eat a thing. I just prayed for my son and for strength. Day three arrived and there was no change in his condition. My sister urged me to take a break and get some fresh air and something to eat but I did not want to miss a second with my son. I didn't know how long I had with him and I didn't want to waste any of it sleeping or eating.

About lunchtime on the third day – I know because my husband left the room to grab some tea and a snack – I was left sitting alone by my son's heated bed. I remember thinking that I hadn't given him a name yet and promised the angels that I would call him Michael, after my dad who had died the year. While I was sitting beside him in the neonatal intensive care unit I prayed again: the strongest, hardest prayer I could muster. I prayed for the angels to save Michael's life.

All of a sudden I felt a gentle but firm squeeze on my left shoulder. I looked around but there was no one there. By now my heart was beating really loud – so loud that I was convinced everyone in the room could hear. Then the beating got softer and calmer and my heart felt warm and strong. I felt peaceful. I looked at Michael. He had a little smile on his tiny face and I knew that even if Michael died the angels would take care of him. Once again I felt a strong squeeze on my left shoulder. I knew then that my prayers were heard and love was surrounding me and my son. I grabbed a cushion and rested my head against the back of my chair. Closing my eyes I fell into a deep sleep.

The next moment I woke up with a start. The life support monitor was making a noise. My son was breathing. Staff circled around but I remained calmly in my seat. I knew that Michael wasn't going anywhere. He was here to stay.

Two weeks later my son made a complete recovery. The doctors were unable to explain how or why but I know exactly why. The angels touched my heart and my son's heart to give us healing and strength. My son is 15 years old now and even though he's more of a little devil than an angel at times I know he is meant to be here.

Many people who have encountered an angel feel an amazing rush of energy, understanding and purpose that changes their lives forever.

For Jenny the experience happened in childhood but it began to fade when she got older and life got more complicated. Eventually, the only way for her to get angels back into her life again was through the power of prayer.

Forever and Ever

When I was about ten years old I went to a strict and very religious primary school. We had to remember a lot of prayers and scriptures. I found it really tedious and boring and I didn't pay much attention. I was much more interested in playtime and learning stuff.

I remember one morning we were saying the Lord's Prayer at assembly in the usual monotone mumble. I got about halfway through and then thought to myself, 'What am I saying? None of this means anything to me.' I looked around at everybody muttering with vacant expressions on their faces and wondered what we were all doing. Later that day we started to learn about angels in the Bible and once again I started to question and to wonder if there really was such a thing as God and angels.

I lay in bed that night trying to go to sleep but then this incredible thing happened, an experience I can't really express in words, a vision of love that I can't really describe. Sparkly, white lights began to surround me like a sky of diamonds and the purest, clearest light imaginable poured love into me, filling me with strength and hope. I sat up and at the end of my bed caught a glimpse of a white gown and wings that were so white. I crawled towards the light but as I did it became a mist. When I got up it disappeared and everything was pitch black again. I wasn't afraid. Talking about my vision now all these years later still sends shivers down my spine.

It was the middle of the night and I didn't want to wake anyone so I curled up in bed and drifted off to sleep. When I woke up in the morning I knew that an angel had visited me. I told my mum and dad and they just smiled but I could tell they didn't believe me. I told my brothers and they said I was crazy. I realized that people weren't going to believe me even though I knew what I had seen was real. I decided not to tell my teachers and my friends and to keep quiet about it. I haven't told another person until now.

I continued to recite prayers and scriptures at school because I had to but they didn't speak to me. I would often wonder at school as we gathered for prayers if anyone really felt what they were saying. The only prayers that would mean anything to me from now on were the prayers spoken by my own heart. I knew I had seen an angel that night when I had doubted their existence.

Fast forward forty years.

I was married by now with two teenage children and a career in advertising that ate up all my free time and my energy. I simply didn't have the time or space to draw strength from my vision or ask the angels for guidance. I had an affair with my boss that cost me my marriage and eventually my job. For a year my kids wouldn't speak to me. My husband remarried. I was in a really lonely place. Mum and dad had passed and my brothers had emigrated to Australia so there wasn't really anyone for me to lean on for support. I only had myself and all the time in the world to reflect on what had gone so wrong with my life.

It was only when I hit rock bottom that I realized what had been missing all these years, what had driven me to seek excitement in a meaningless affair and to work all those long hours neglecting my kids. I had forgotten about the angels. I started to speak to them again from the bottom on my heart and as soon as I did my situation improved. I found a new job that didn't require me to sweat blood. My eldest son got in touch with me again and after some time my youngest son moved back in with me for a few years while he studied for his law exams. I even started dating again.

Today, I don't let a day go by without asking my angels for guidance and support. I believe there are angels all around me. It isn't the same as when I was a child. I can't see angels now but I feel them. It feels magical … almost like that heady feeling when you fall in love for the first time.

It's awesome when you've been touched by an angel. The adrenaline rush is out of this world. I felt like I could walk on air after I heard my mother speaking to me in spirit when my second child was born. But, as the years have marched by since then, and the routine of my daily life has set in again, it's sometimes hard to keep the memory fresh and alive. When I sense it fading I do all I can to remember and recall, but sometimes this isn't enough. That's where prayer or silent meditation can be so rewarding because it refreshes my memory by reminding me of the constant presence of angels in my life.

Just Believe

Working on this book hasn't always been easy. Although I've been overwhelmed by the number of courageous and wonderful people willing to contribute their stories my efforts have also been undermined by those who refuse to accept that angels exist. Some say, 'Angels aren't real. It's just nonsense.' Others say, 'There's no proof.' Many more say, 'Get real.'

Angels are astonishing beings with incredible powers but what many doubters fail to understand is that angels are spiritual not physical beings. They exist in an entirely different time and space to us and this difference makes it hard for us to imagine how something so very different to our own existence can be real. But even though our minds are too limited to ever fully understand them, angels are real. And for those who ask for proof, surely the countless stories from people all over the world who have been touched by angels are proof enough.

Tim didn't believe in angels but, as he explains below, a boy with a broken arm changed his perspective.

Turn Around

I have very little memory of being attacked. All I can remember is waking up in hospital with bandages all over my arms and face and the taste of blood in my mouth. Apparently I had been putting cash into my wallet after visiting the cashpoint when I was attacked from behind by a group of yobs. I must have put up a fight because they didn't get my wallet or my cash. I'd been saved by a lady walking her dog; she came round the corner and set the dog on them.

Anyway, I was due to be discharged from hospital in a day or two when I met this boy, he must have been about 14 or 15. He had broken his arm but this wasn't the worst of it. He had fallen off his dad's motorcycle and shattered his arm in twelve different places. Gangrene was setting in and there was a strong chance he would lose his arm. The saddest thing was that he was a talented pianist. I liked this boy so when he asked me to come with him to the chapel and pray for the angels to heal his arm I was fine about it.

I wheeled him down to the chapel and sat quietly as he bowed his head in prayer. I sat a few feet back from him feeling a bit uncomfortable. I was a realist and believing in angels didn't make sense to me.

After a few minutes the boy turned round and asked me to join him. I hadn't prayed since I was at school and didn't feel at all comfortable but the boy insisted. Clearly it was important to him so I bowed my head and thought about the boy. I really focused on his arm. In my mind's eye I saw him fully recovered and playing the piano to an appreciative audience.

The next day I was discharged. I asked about the boy and heard that he had been operated on and his arm had been saved. I went to visit him a week later and the first thing he said was. 'I knew you would save my arm. That's why we met.' I told him that it was the brilliance of the doctors and the hospitals that had saved him, not me, but he shook his head and said it was also the both of us working together.

If I hadn't ended up in hospital I might never have met this kid. Perhaps I was there to pray for and believe in him. Perhaps meeting this boy was the only way for the angels to show me they are real. In hospital I guess I was his.

We should always respond to any urge to help or comfort others, whether it be an inner one or one urged upon us by others, even if we aren't sure why. As Laura's story further illustrates, empathy for others can have an awesome power.

The Last Hope

Karen worked in the same office as me. She was always cheerful and friendly even when she got passed over for promotion. I had no idea she was deeply unhappy.

Every morning I'd have a quick chat with Karen as we got our obligatory caffeine fix. Nothing deep or serious: she'd ask me how I was, I'd ask her how she was and then we might talk films or what we planned to do that evening – usual 'friends but not quite friends' kind of chat. However, one morning as she was making her cuppa I noticed something different about her. What was it? I felt that she was sad but she wasn't behaving unusually or anything, just sniffing the milk to make sure it wasn't off and filing the kettle with water the same way she had done for years. Still, I sensed something around her. It's hard to describe but the more I looked the more I seemed to see a pale light folding around her, like an aura. The glow was particularly strong around her chest as if it was some kind of force protecting her, but from what? There wasn't anything dangerous here. I closed my eyes to refocus but still I saw the light. I was even more astonished when other people walked past or talked to her and didn't seem to notice.

All day I couldn't stop thinking about her. My eyes kept drifting in her direction to see if the aura was still there and it was. I kept feeling this sadness and praying that Karen wasn't feeling it.

By the end of the day the aura had faded but as I put on my hat and coat ready to leave I was in a quandary. Should I tell Karen what I had seen? It's really hard to do things like that because people are always going to think you are a bit odd. I decided not to say anything but as I stepped into the lift something made me jump out and head back to her desk.

Karen was still working as I approached her desk. Several letters were lined up on her desk and she was putting another one in an envelope. She looked really tired and told me she'd be packing up soon and going home. I gently sat down beside her and blurted out what

I had seen. I said, 'I believe you are blessed. An angel has been with you all day, holding you in strong, protective arms.'

Karen stared at me for several seconds, without uttering a word. I was just about to beat a hasty retreat and apologize if I had upset her when I noticed that her eyes were filling up with tears. I gave her a tissue. It was then that she shared with me her terrible news.

The letters on her desk were farewell letters for her colleagues to discover the next morning. She was planning to take her life. A year ago she had lost her youngest son, Joshua, in the war in Iraq and had struggled to find meaning ever since. But now that I had told her an angel was watching over her she wondered if this was the sign she had been longing for. She went on to tell me that she had asked for a sign and my words felt like an enormous weight was lifting from her heart – she realized that she didn't want to die. She had something to believe in now. She had hope.

After that day Karen's life changed dramatically. We've been the best of friends ever since. She signed up to train as a bereavement counsellor and recently left her job to set up her own counselling practice. She feels that her depression had a purpose after all. It helped her develop patience and tenderness for others whose lives have also been shattered by grief and the loss of a loved one. She's recently become a grandmother as well and her daughter has named her little son Joshua, after his uncle.

It's incredible how many times I've had a phone call from a friend after they've been in my thoughts and I've sent them happy ones. It's almost as if they have heard me. It's the same for those who have lost a loved one: praying for them really does help and strengthen them. Remember, I'm not recommending that you get down on bended knee – cards, phone calls, well wishes, flowers, angel poems or figures, your time, listening, or happy, positive thoughts sent in their direction will do the job just as well.

In the following story, Jack's prayers were for something that appeared quite trivial at the time; but later turned out to be absolutely crucial.

Clear Vision

A bunch of us went down to the beach to soak up the sun. It was a glorious day and the beach was surprisingly empty apart from a couple of mums shouting at their kids to be careful. I was napping on the blanket while my mates Don and Devon went splashing in the ocean. About an hour later Don came up to me looking terribly upset. He said a huge wave had knocked him off balance and he had lost his glasses. He had been searching with

Devon for about 20 minutes already. Devon had a pair of goggles and had been diving but found nothing. I asked Don where he had lost his spectacles and we walked down towards the shore.

I swam out and realized it was impossible. Even though the ocean water was clear today, with the lapping waves moving me around and the sand kicking up under the water, I couldn't see anything. I asked to borrow Devon's goggles. It was like looking for a needle in a haystack. I couldn't see anything. The goggles only allowed me to see right in front like tunnel vision and I could only hold my breath for about 30 seconds tops. All I could do was look straight down with the limited view from the goggles, moving to different spots each time, as I had no idea if I was even searching in the right area.

I felt really sorry for Don because he was as blind as a bat without his glasses. The next bus back to the city was in four hours and he would have to sit on the beach all that time doing nothing. Don needed this day more than the rest of us. His sister suffered from Down's syndrome and because his mum had to work Don was her main carer for most of the summer holidays. Today was his first day off all summer. Standing waist deep with the goggles tight over my face, I prayed silently that I would find the spectacles and dived in again.

Suddenly, right there in front of my eyes were the glasses. I could barely see them as the water was cloudy from the sand and the frames were wire thin. I could see the waves coming through the sand and was worried that a wave would push the glasses out of my field of vision. I knew I had to act quickly because if I went up for air, I would probably lose sight of them. I remember thinking, 'If I can only reach them.'

I stretched my hand towards the glasses and barely touched them and after a bit more stretching, was finally able to grab them. I couldn't believe that I got them in my hands. It seemed like forever.

When I came up for air with the glasses held up triumphantly in my hand Devon and Don rushed over towards me. They told me that I had been under for several minutes and they were starting to panic. I've never held my breath for more than a minute before.

Don was thrilled to have his glasses back and we spent the rest of the time getting sunburned.

A few hours later as we waited with a mum and her noisy kids for the bus to pick us up and take us home, Devon and I whiled away the time playing on our portable play stations. Don wasn't as crazy about gaming as we were but was happy to sit quietly and cool down in the shade as we all looked like lobsters.

I was just about to break through to level three on my game when it flew out of my hands. Don had knocked into me when without warning he shot out of his seat and pulled a little girl – aged about three or four – back onto the pavement moments before a motorbike flew past. Without doubt, if Don hadn't grabbed her she would have died as her mum was busy putting suncream on her shoulders and wasn't paying attention.

The mother grabbed a reluctant Don in her arms and thanked him from the bottom of her heart for saving her daughter from injury and possibly death. Perhaps in earnest – or perhaps in an attempt to untangle himself from her sweaty embrace – Don looked at me and winked. 'Don't thank me,' he said. 'Thank him. If he hadn't found my glasses today I'd have never seen that bike in time.'

I believe the angels heard my prayer that day. They helped me find those spectacles because Don would need them later to save a little girl's life.

If Jack hadn't prayed to find those glasses a little girl may have died. His story shows that even the most trivial and apparently unimportant things can have an importance that is impossible to measure or predict at the time. Seen in this light nothing we say, do or think is ever insignificant or trivial in the eyes of an angel and every selfless act or deed has a ripple effect that sometimes we can witness but other times we can't.

Distance is no object when it comes to the healing power of prayer. Separated from his pregnant sister by hundreds of thousands of miles and unable to help when she got sick, Brian did the only thing he could.

A Hole in the Heart

I want to share this story about my sister. We were always close but when our father and mother both died in a car crash when I was 13 and she was 11 our bond became unbreakable. We clung to each other. People could say how sorry they were and offer sympathy but no one else could really understand how it felt to be a carefree child one day and an orphan the next.

My aunt and uncle stepped in to take care of both of us. They told us that mum and dad were being looked after by the angels but I didn't believe them. When something so tragic and unjust happens it is hard to believe in angels. Night after night I would sob myself to sleep cradling my sister in my arms. As the years drifted away the grief wasn't so intense but there was a hole in my heart that I felt would never heal.

It was tough for me when my sister got married as I knew I wasn't going to be the first man in her life any more, but above all I wanted her to be happy. I know she was worried about how I would react but I assured her I would be okay. And I was. Married or not I knew my sister would always be there for me. I also knew that as close as we were, we both had our own lives to lead so when I got offered a job abroad a month later I decided to go for it.

There were tears and hugs but also smiles at the airport as I left. I was starting an exciting new phase in my life.

Both of us promised to email and call with our news as much as we could. We both kept our promise. Almost every evening I would go online and send or read emails to my sister and if we were online at the same time we would send instant messages.

I was delighted when I heard that my sister was pregnant. Every thing was routine with the pregnancy until about 22 weeks. I remember the evening very clearly. We were both talking to each other via computer. I asked her how she was and she said that she was starting to have real problems – swelling, headaches and vomiting. I could sense my sister was scared. I offered to fly out but she said she was fine.

The next day, Andrew, her husband called to say she was being airlifted to a hospital that dealt with neonatal emergencies. I had no contact with her for the next 12 hours. I was frantic with worry and booked myself on the first available flight the following day. In the night Alan called to tell me that my dear little niece had gone to heaven. To say I was heartbroken for him was an understatement. I cannot explain how devastated I felt for my sister's loss.

Then the words came … the words I had heard once before and never wanted to hear again. 'She may not make it either.' I felt like my heart and soul had died at that very moment. I had heard similar words when my mum and dad were fighting for their lives all those years ago and neither of them had pulled through. What could I do thousands of miles away? Well, the only thing I knew to do was to pray with all my heart and soul.

I found something I thought I had lost forever that night, something I had buried long ago. I got my faith back again even though I was tormented with the possible loss of my sister. I knew my guardian angel heard every word that came from my mouth and sensed every tear I shed. I could feel my angel repairing the hole in my heart and soul. I knew I wasn't alone.

Then something miraculous happened.

The following morning when I arrived at the hospital I heard the only words I wanted to hear. My sister had returned to us. She was broken, hurt and shattered with grief at the loss of her baby but she had returned just the same. I couldn't see her until the evening as she needed to rest but I felt as if I was walking on air. I prayed to the angels to give her strength to recover from her loss.

When I sat by her bedside that evening she told me everything. She had coded out – died – twice and been resuscitated twice. Most incredible of all she knew exactly what was happening each time. Both times she felt herself leaving her body and gently floating to a warm and comforting light. She wanted to go as she could feel mum and dad close by her but both times she heard a voice calling her back – it was my voice. She heard me praying word for word. The second time she didn't only hear my prayers but the prayers of her husband and everyone who loved her. She listened to all our prayers and came home to us.

This happened five years ago and my sister is now the proud mother of twins. There have been quite a few changes in my life too. I've met someone special and have been happily married for a year. We haven't been blessed with children yet but I look forward to the day. I wanted to share this story to let as many people as possible know that angels are among us and they are protecting us and listening to our prayers.

There was more than one miracle that happened here. First and foremost, my sister came back to us and second, the faith I had lost ever since my parents died returned. I am thankful for the experience, even though it took a tragedy for me to give my heart back to the angels.

Coincidences

There are times when the angels don't answer us directly, but in a way sceptics would call just a coincidence.

How many times has this happened to you? You are thinking of someone, the mobile rings and there is a text from them? Or have you ever found yourself in the right place at exactly the right time? Is this a coincidence or an answered prayer?

The dictionary defines coincidences as 'striking chance occurrences'. But when these happen to us we simply have to ask, 'Is that all there is to it?' It feels like something so much more and few of us can dismiss what Carl Jung called 'synchronistic phenomena' so easily.

Coincidences that have a major impact on your life – saving it or turning it around – certainly suggest power from a higher source. Because our human minds are limited, a coincidence can seem like mere chance. For example, hearing a song that seems to speak directly to you or meeting someone who transforms your life. But if we stop trying to analyse and question and simply acknowledge that something magnificent is in tune with us when coincidences occur our lives can be transformed.

In recent years a book, *The Celestine Prophecy*, which became a runaway and surprise bestseller, suggested that people and the world are guided towards a higher purpose and that the first way to become conscious of this movement forward is to tap into the coincidences in our lives. In the book author, James Redfield, hints that if everyone begins to take coincidences seriously, paying attention to what they are and what they mean, humankind will progress to an advanced stage of evolution.

Millions of people have been inspired by the book and although I didn't agree with every one of its insights I applaud the author for highlighting a higher power behind coincidence and encouraging people to focus more intensely on the deeper meaning of coincidences in their lives.

Coincidences have played a huge part in shaping my life and I hope they will continue to do so. One of the greatest joys of getting older is looking back with hindsight and seeing how neatly things have stacked into place in your life. Even though I wasn't aware of it at the time, every experience I have had has brought me to the place I am now. Think about the people who are touching your life right now. What amazing coincidences have brought you all together? Think about all the situations in your life when things just seemed to fall together perfectly. What other coincidences are out there waiting for you to find them?

Over the years I've learned that the more I become aware of coincidences and the more I express appreciation for them the more likely I am to encounter them in my life. Feelings of gratitude have a truly awesome power in the world of spirit and invite magical coincidences and angels into your life.

After considering all that I have experienced, read and been told about coincidences over the years it is my firm belief that angels can sometimes help us in ways that transcend what we think of as normal. I believe that in coincidences the angels are calling out to us. And to understand what they are trying to say all we need to do is listen to them, trust them and thank them.

Like countless other people who have been encouraged, inspired, saved or comforted by the miracle of coincidences, Lucy is in no doubt that a higher power was making decisions for her.

Everything Seemed to Fall into Place

About ten years ago now my partner Steve and I were on a two-week holiday in Crete. As you do on holiday we soon established a routine for ourselves; the beach in the morning followed by lunch and a nap and then some sightseeing in the afternoon.

On the seventh day we woke up and I realized that we had forgotten to do our laundry the day before. We were out of clean towels and swimming costumes. So we went to the laundry in the morning instead of the beach. When we got there we saw a big sign saying the owners would be back in one hour. Determined not to let this spoil our fun we decided to do a bit of sightseeing. We drove down a road we hadn't been down before and found ourselves in a really remote area. The beach there was stunning and virtually deserted. It was so inviting that we decided to skip our nap and after collecting our laundry and eating lunch head up there.

That afternoon, when we got back to the beach, we put down our towels and started applying suncream. A man suddenly ran in our direction screaming. He was shouting and pointing to a child being carried by a woman from the ocean. I could see that the child was unconscious and I longed to be able to help. People were gathering around and everyone was shouting, but I stayed put because I didn't want to add to the panic.

And then I remembered something very important. A few weeks before going on holiday I had completed a first-aid course. I had learned how to do basic CPR or cardiopulmonary resuscitation. Without hesitation I ran over with my blanket, asked the man to put the girl down and started CPR. Steve phoned for an ambulance. At first there was no response from the girl but I kept going for what seemed like forever. Then she opened her eyes, spat out water and started to moan. I kept going with the CPR until the ambulance arrived. Later I was told that she made a complete recovery.

I've often thought back to that day when everything just seemed to fall into place as if by magic. First of all, we never forget to do our laundry on time. Secondly, if we hadn't forgotten our laundry we would never have visited that beach. Thirdly, we always swim in the mornings on holiday and not in the afternoon. Fourthly, I had only completed the office first-aid course because I'd been asked to. I hadn't volunteered to do it. The person who had agreed to do it had phoned in sick that week. If you add all these things up it has to be more than pure coincidence.

Sometimes angels will bring people into our lives at exactly the right time. This 'right time, right place' phenomenon has happened to me so many times I don't even call it a phenomenon any more, I call it life. For Beth, the chance appearance of an old school friend was beyond coincidence.

A Mother's Pleading Prayer

My son, Connor, was surfing mad. One day he went surfing with a group of his friends. He came back complaining that his legs and back hurt because the waves had been particularly strong. I thought nothing of it but by morning the pain was so bad I rushed him to hospital. The doctors took a look at him and said it was just muscle strain. The pain would probably go in a week or two and in the meantime he should rest and definitely stay away from water sports of any kind.

Connor listened to their advice and took it easy but instead of easing, the pain got worse. After about two weeks Connor was in such pain that he wouldn't leave his bedroom. I came in one morning with breakfast and saw that he had been crying. I prayed that his pain would ease soon and took comfort in the thought that the doctor had said he would feel better in a week or two.

The next day I got an email which nearly knocked me sideways. Louise, a friend of mine from junior school, was passing through town. She'd looked me up on friends reunited and wondered if I'd like to meet her. It had been nearly 30 years since I had last seen her and happy memories of playground antics flashed through my mind. Of course I wanted to meet her. She suggested we meet at the station but remembering that Connor was poorly and might need me I gave her my address and invited her round for a cup of tea instead.

When Louise called round it was as if the years in between had disappeared and we didn't stop talking and laughing and drinking tea for an hour or two. I'm ashamed to admit it but I almost forgot that Connor was upstairs so when he stumbled downstairs with his face crumbled up in pain I felt incredibly guilty. As soon as Louise saw Connor she asked me if she could examine him. I was fine about it as she had told me she was a qualified nurse with years of experience. She had a feel of his lower back and then told us both that she didn't like what she saw and that Connor should go to hospital immediately.

At hospital Louise insisted that Connor have X-rays and a series of tests. To cut a long story short there were signs of infection and he had to be operated on that day. The operation was successful and the surgeon told me that if we had waited just one or two more days Connor, my sports mad son, may have been wheelchair bound for the rest of his life.

Call this a coincidence or whatever but in my mind when I prayed for Connor the angels sent Louise to my house. For Connor and for me Louise is a walking miracle.

Coincidences that answer the prayers of loved ones looking for a reassuring sign have the power to bring extraordinary comfort and healing. Christina's story is a delightful example.

A Dog's Tale

I was only 22 when I lost the love of my life, Robin, in a freak skiing accident. We had planned to get married in a couple of years. Night after night I cried my eyes out. I curled up in a ball, wrenching with grief and pain and praying I would get a sign from him. There was only silence.

After the funeral I tried to get my life back together but I felt like I was just going through the paces. Something inside me had died and something inside me didn't really want to live. I visited the cemetery once, twice, three and four times a day. I'd beg and plead for a sign. Just one glimpse of him to let me know he was still here. I even asked if he could come back as a dog; we were both dog lovers but had never been able to buy one because our rented flat was a pet-free zone. We promised ourselves that when we got married and had a house of our own and enough money it would be littered with dogs.

One morning when I woke up very early and couldn't get back to sleep I decided to go the cemetery to have some special time alone with Robin. I spoke to myself as I went there, 'Robin, it's early in the morning. No one else will be around. Please give me a sign. I need a sign.'

My visit there was incredibly emotional. I wanted to hold him and to hug him one last time. I put a sausage roll on top of his headstone. About a year before he had died I had eaten a sausage roll from the fridge that he had unsuccessfully hidden for a midnight feast. Later he told me he had searched for that sausage roll feverishly and fruitlessly that night. The sausage roll episode had become a joke for us ever since.

Picture the scene. It's very early in the morning and I'm talking to a gravestone and giving it a sausage roll. Within moments birds swoop down and perch nearby ready to attack the roll. Then out of nowhere a stray dog came running up to me. It looked fierce. I was scared. Then it just stopped and stared at me with eyes that reminded me of Robin's. It looked at the sausage roll, licking its lips. I threw the roll to the floor and the dog picked it up and trotted to me. When it got to me it stopped growling and sat down to eat it. It even let me stroke it. Then when the sausage roll had disappeared the dog licked my hand and sped away. I have never seen that dog before or since.

A coincidence? Not to me. I truly believe that Robin sent this dog to make me smile. He finally got that sausage roll! My encounter with the dog that day gave me such a profound sense of comfort and hope that I want to share with all those who have lost loved ones. I've moved on with my life now and am opening my heart again in another special relationship. Loving someone again feels so right I know that Robin is happy for me.

I truly believe that loved ones can help us from the other side but they tend to do so in ways that can often only be interpreted personally. Like Christina, Ruby asked for a sign and the angels heard her.

Paint a Rainbow

Charlotte was only four years old when she died. I think about her every second of every day. I miss her every time my heart beats but the grief and torment I felt has been replaced by a sense of comfort. Let me explain.

Charlotte was fantastic at drawing for one so young. She was forever scribbling and handing me pictures of stick men and women. In the months before she died she'd include rainbows in almost all of her pictures. She's even draw snowmen with rainbows hovering over them. When I asked her why she just smiled and said that you can have rainbows anywhere you wanted to.

I don't want to go into the details of her unexpected death as some things are too personal but I do want to tell you about her funeral. I woke up on the day of her funeral numb with shock and aching with grief. My mum had to help me get dressed as I was shaking so much and could barely stand. I wanted my little girl back. I would have given my life to have my little girl back. I regretted all those times I had sent her back to bed when she couldn't sleep. Why hadn't I held her; savoured every precious second? I longed for some kind of sign from her that she was okay and that she was in a place where there was only love and joy. I prayed for a sign.

It was raining hard as we drove towards the church but I barely noticed. Everything seemed bleak and grey now; the world had lost its colour without her in it and even if the sun had been out it would still have felt like rain to me. We stood there with our umbrellas as her little coffin was lowered into the grave. My legs felt weak and I sank to the ground sobbing. People gathered round to help me up but I didn't want to get up. I wanted to sink into the earth.

It was my mother who forced me to look up. She lifted my chin and told me to open my eyes and there was the most stunning rainbow I have ever seen. The colours were vivid, bright and intense and the more I looked at it the more the colours sparkled. The rainbow was so lovely I knew it was Charlotte speaking to me. I got up and looked over at the street that ran past the cemetery. People were stopping their cars and getting out of them to gaze at the rainbow. I've never seen a rainbow so intense and colourful since.

The world stood still for me that moment and colour came back into my life again. I hugged my two other children and told them that wherever we were in the world Charlotte would be with us, smiling down on us, reminding us that you can see rainbows anywhere.

Of course, some people might interpret this story differently, but any person who has lost a child or a loved one will know different. When the angels see the pain of a grieving parent they can pour comfort into our hearts by showing us that those we have lost are here with us right now, in every bit of creation.

I have had many personal experiences which convince me that we are surrounded by signs that the angels take an interest in our day-to-day lives, giving us a reassuring sign or helping hand when we need it. And this help isn't just of a spiritual kind; the angels can be surprisingly practical, as Kate explains.

Mysterious Ways

Back in the mid-eighties I was fresh out of college and broke. When my mum died in my first year at college I had felt totally alone in the world. I just about survived through college, working as a waitress in the evening and living in college digs. The plan was to get a job in arts administration as soon as possible after graduation.

I had just about enough money saved to survive for a month but if I didn't get a job soon I'd have to waitress full time instead of part time simply to pay the rent. My mum had left me no money and I was too timid – or is it proud? – to ask my friends for help. I had three interviews lined up that month and I *had* to get one of them.

The first interview didn't go well at all; I felt hopelessly outclassed by the other candidates and my lack of confidence worked against me. My second interview went better but I still missed out. With just one more job interview before my money ran out I knew that I would have to give it my all. I longed to get my hair done and buy a new outfit or pair of shoes. I desperately needed a confidence boost. I'd been wearing charity shop clothes for so long now I didn't even know what new clothes looked or felt like.

I was in my room the afternoon before the interview trying to feel optimistic when the doorbell rang. A woman with a kind face asked me if I had any clothing I wanted to contribute to a clothing drive. I didn't have anything except for a few items still hanging in my wardrobe that belonged to my mum; a couple of dresses and an overcoat that my mum wore so much I used to call it her second skin. I'd have worn it too if it hadn't been way too big for me; my mum had been a great deal taller than me.

I'd clung on to the dresses and coat ever since my mum had died but for some reason now seemed the right time to let them go. I went to my wardrobe, folded them neatly and gave them to the woman.

An hour or so later the doorbell rang again. It was the same woman and she asked me if my name was Kate. When I said it was she handed me an envelope saying it had been in my mum's old overcoat. The envelope was large and I wondered why I hadn't noticed it or even felt it. When I opened the envelope I couldn't believe my eyes. There was a wad of money inside and when I added it up, the total came to just over £1,000.

Needless to say, I booked an appointment at the hairdresser immediately and treated myself to a brand new pair of killer heels, a suit and a jacket. I felt a million dollars and breezed through my interview. The job was offered to me on the spot.

You could say that the clothes and shoes gave me the confidence boost I needed at the right time but for me what really made the difference was mum looking out for me and helping me from the other side. It was like she was saying one last time, 'I believe in you. It's high time you started believing in yourself.'

I often used to hesitate to ask angels for practical help, especially money, believing that any material needs contaminated my spiritual needs. Well, more and more over the years I have learned that the angels do sometimes help in practical ways. Often this comes in the form of 'coincidental' surprise gifts, including money, being given to someone in need at exactly the right time.

On more than one occasion I've found myself at the receiving end of a surprise gift when I really needed help. Once, when money was particularly tight when I first went to live in London I found £3,000 in an envelope in the street.

Another time, about 15 years ago, when I was trying to establish myself as a journalist and just about scraping by financially, I met a guy at a party who was working in the same town that I had lived in for about four years when I was in my teens. We chatted for a while about the town and its local theatre. I thought nothing of it until six months later when a mutual friend told me that this guy had called her and said he had seen an ad in the local paper with my name in it urging me to get in touch with a local solicitor. I did so immediately and was told that I had been left a tidy sum in the will of a man called Mr Rosin.

I had worked for Mr Rosin for about a year just before I headed off to university. He was severely disabled but he had a sharp mind and incredible determination. After running errands for him I would often stay longer than I should to chat and I looked forward to visiting him every week. Despite his disability he was doing so much for others; working as a volunteer accountant for local charities and teaching at the local business college. He was an inspiration.

When I left for university my family moved again and I gradually lost touch with Mr Rosin. You can imagine then what a massive shock his gift was after all those years – he hadn't seemed like a wealthy man.

There's not a day that goes past that I don't thank him and feel inspired by his determination to make a difference with his life. Mr Rosin was an angel, regardless of the money. But if it hadn't been for the coincidence of bumping into a guy who happened to read the local papers in the town where I once lived I might never have found out about his gift to me.

Apparent coincidences can not only bring comfort, healing, reassurance and even practical help in times of need they can, as Sarah's story below shows, also help people find their way out of the darkness.

New Dawn

My husband was the CEO of a major corporation and I was a successful photographer in my own right. We lived in a large house in one of the most expensive parts of Bath, received invitations to every party in town and had enough money to indulge every whim.

Everyone saw me as this hugely successful woman with a strong marriage in total control of everything in her life. And in many ways, I was. I had it all – the career, the husband, money and plans for kids one day – I was very happy with my life. But if I look back now, there were signs all along that something wasn't right.

I started to have days when I would find myself crying for no reason. I put it down to hormones, as I suffered from terrible PMS, but now I think it was a warning sign of the depression that was to come.

Despite this glittering life everyone thought I was living, I felt constantly sad. Trouble was I couldn't admit to anyone how I felt. If you are successful and everyone envies you how can you admit something feels wrong? Admitting to feeling depressed would have been an admission of failure, that there was something wrong with me. Even worse, people would have labelled me a spoiled brat; I was acutely aware that I had so much and there were so many people with 'real' reasons to be depressed out there.

Around this time my photographic work was propelling me into the spotlight. I was urged to do celebrity shoots and attend fashion shows but my heart wasn't in it. It didn't mean anything to me. I stopped sleeping and eating properly. I had dark circles under my eyes and my clothes were all too big. I lost weight because every time I tried to eat I got a lump in my throat and would start to cry.

My husband moved out. My depression was only partly to blame as things hadn't been good between us for a while. When he left the house fell silent. I'd wake up every night at exactly 2.40 am with a rush of thoughts going through my head. I managed to just about keep it together at work, but when I got home I'd cry endlessly. I put it down to my divorce. I took a two-week vacation in the sun but cut it short by a week because I spent the entire time crying behind my sunglasses.

Eventually, I paid a visit to my doctor and he prescribed anti-depressants but they didn't work. I went for counselling and that made me cry even more. It became harder and harder to put up a show of normality and eventually I was fired. Fortunately, my divorce settlement meant that I had no financial worries but losing my job was the final blow.

I felt totally separated from life and from other people. I would wander around the city with my dark glasses on crying and watching other people get on with their lives and feeling completely out of touch with anyone or anything. The woman I'd once been – the woman who had it all – had vanished. Now even simple things like getting up in the morning and washing my hair felt impossible. I hardly left my house, stopped washing, wearing make-up or cleaning my teeth, and ate virtually nothing. Any essentials I couldn't do without I would order online and have delivered to my door.

None of the medication or therapy I was prescribed worked, so I turned to the bottle. I drank two bottles of wine a day. It numbed the pain. Then one night I gathered together all the pills in my house and decided to take them all along with a bottle of gin. I didn't even count them or see what they were; I just decided I was going to take the lot. As I started to take the pills one by one all I could think was, 'Please God, let it be over. I want to be free now.'

Then the doorbell rang. I ignored it and popped another pill into my mouth but it rang again and again and again. This person wasn't going away. I looked out of the window and it was the postman; of course, he wasn't going away because he knew I was always in. I staggered downstairs and opened the door. He gave me a parcel and then told me he needed some money to pay for a letter that had insufficient postage on it. This had never happened before and I told him to forget it and come back tomorrow. He looked at me and said smiling, 'Fine by me love, tomorrow's another day.'

When I shut the door I sank to the floor with my head in my hands. The postman's words had triggered something in me. My name is Sarah but my middle name is Scarlett. My mum had named me Scarlett after the plucky heroine Scarlett O'Hara in *Gone with the Wind*. 'Tomorrow is another day,' were Scarlett's famous last words in the film;

even when all appeared lost and her husband walked out on her she still had hope. Was some higher power sending me a message?

At that moment a ray of sunlight shone through the window onto my face. I felt a surge of energy, peace and comfort. For the first time in years I didn't want to cry. I wanted to get up and dance. Although it was late afternoon it felt like a glorious new dawn to me. That day was the end of my drinking and my depression and the beginning of my new life.

Even though that day was a turning point my recovery was slow and not easy and I had to start with the smallest of things but eventually I began to find meaning in my life again. I downsized my house, got a new job working for a charity, and started opening my heart to other people again. To this day I remember the words of that postman. I believe they were heaven sent by an angel who loved me enough to make me see that although I was stuck in a dark place there was always hope.

When Sarah was at her lowest the angels sent her a powerful message triggered by the 'coincidence' of a postman's chance remark and her middle name. Her story and all the stories in this chapter show that you don't need to worship angels to be blessed by their love and guidance. All you need to do is ask and they will hear as long as your request comes from the heart.

So be careful what you ask for! Ask the angels to set you on the right path. Ask for strength and comfort during the tough times. Ask them to bring you love and guidance. Ask them to create magic in your life but, above all, ask them to be there by your side. With angels in your heart and in your life you are never alone.

CHAPTER 4

Celestial Rescues

They will lift you in their hands so that you will not
strike your foot against a stone.

Psalm 91

Brace yourself: the stories in this chapter and the next are
a matter of life and death so expect them to cut a little
deeper into your soul than heart-warming stories of
unexplained scents or invisible kisses. It's astonishing
enough when a mysterious sign or event unexpectedly
turns your life around or your prayers are answered, but
when the life of a loved one or your own life has been
saved miraculously, the wonder of it can be overpowering.

After my life was spared ten years ago by a warning
given in a dream, I was completely overwhelmed and
buzzing with energy. There was so much I wanted to do
with my life and I wasn't going to waste another
precious second. There is nothing like the possibility of
death to wake us up to the beauty of life. But we don't

have to wait for that shock. You don't need a brush with death to start doing all the things you have wanted to do with your life. What are you waiting for? You can start doing them all right now!

The accounts you'll read in this chapter go way beyond coincidence. In every true account something totally astonishing occurs that seems to either prevent or direct those involved away from certain tragedy. Curiously, many of these celestial rescues are also spontaneous; they aren't planned, prayed for or even yearned for because in most cases there was absolutely no prior knowledge of the threat that lay in wait for them.

But clearly the angels did know what the future held and were able to give a warning. Sometimes this warning was in the form of a powerful feeling or a flash of intuition. Sometimes it came as a whisper or even a shout if that was needed. In some cases the celestial rescues were even more extraordinary.

The explanation of angelic intervention is enough for some people. Others find answers in theories that everything is connected and time is an illusion: there is no past, present or future and our minds can somehow catch a glimpse of the future. Whatever explanation is put forward it's impossible to not be amazed by stories of people whose lives have been saved by angels.

Let's get things started here with Amber's striking account. Seemingly impossible 'nick of time' rescues, like

Amber's, are not the only way for angels to reach into our world and touch our lives. But because the stories are often so dramatic and intense it's not hard to see why they are so compelling and attention grabbing.

Angel in the Sea

I was on holiday with a couple of friends in Barbados. A week had passed and we still had another week to go. It really was like paradise. I'd spend my days sinking into the dazzling white sand, gazing at the turquoise waves calling me in for a soothing swim. I didn't want this holiday to end.

One morning I napped a little too long in the sun and when I woke up I felt in urgent need of a cool down. I woke up my mates and urged them to come into the sea with me but they were intent on topping up their tan. I laughed and ran into the waves. I settled into a steady back stroke for a few minutes but then as I turned round to practise my front crawl I felt a rush of cold water swirl around me. I'd been caught by a current and it was pulling me under. Struggling to keep my head above the water I tried to shout and wave to my friends. To my horror they simply waved back; they thought I was larking about.

The current was too strong for me. My head went under again and again. I was being swept away to sea. My friends finally realized what had happened and

I glimpsed them running for help. But I knew I was beyond help. No one would be able to get to me in time. I sank under the water and images flashed through my mind. I was at school. I was opening Christmas presents. I was passing my driving test. I was at my job interview. I saw my parents. Even though I was underwater I cried out that I wasn't ready to die. My life had barely begun.

I felt a strong arm grip my waist and it pulled my head to the surface. I turned around and saw a middle-aged woman with silver hair supporting me. She told me to swim and out of nowhere I felt the strength returning to my legs. Slowly but surely I swam to shore. I could see my friends swimming towards me, shock etched onto their faces. They grabbed me and pulled me out of the sea. They were in shock because they thought that I had drowned. I turned around to thank my silver-haired saviour but she wasn't there. I asked my friends to tell me where she had gone; I was worried she might be in trouble. But the sea was still and empty. I asked them if they had seen her save my life but they shook their heads and told me they hadn't seen anyone.

As I sat on the sand shivering and chattering about a mysterious woman I'm sure my friends thought I was simply in a state of shock like them but I know different. I thought about the calm and strong woman who had saved me and a feeling of great peace, calm and strength bolted through me. I realized then that it hadn't been a human being that had saved me but an angel. It wasn't my time to die that day.

From that day on my life changed completely. When I came home I knew that my destiny was to help save the lives of others. I retrained as a paramedic. There are many lives of course that I can't save in my job but for those that I do save and for those I don't, I know that an angel is watching.

Amber thought her life was ending that day but now believes it was only beginning. She was drowning and her friends would not have been able to get to her in time to save her but an angel was watching over her.

Like Amber, Tim is also certain that an angel saved him from certain death in a car crash. Here's his story.

An Angel in My Car

It was a Friday evening in the summer of 1979. It's been nearly 30 years but it's something I'll never, ever forget. I was driving behind some of my friends to a party that was out of town. I didn't know the way so had to follow closely behind them in their huge Lincoln town car. Their car was so massive I could barely see around it.

All of a sudden the Lincoln swerved out into the left lane passing a Ford mini-truck who was sitting dead-still in the middle of the road trying to turn left into his driveway.

I slammed on my brakes, tried to steer right but hit his bumper going about 40 miles an hour! My car was a write-off.

Seatbelt use was not a law then, I didn't have one on. But, as I slammed into the back of that truck, I felt powerful hands rest on my shoulders. They held me in my seat. I did not hit the steering wheel, fly through the windshield, or even move out of my seat! The man whose truck I had hit leapt out of his truck and came running over to me. He couldn't believe I was alive. He was so happy to see me alive that he wasn't in the slightest bit angry or upset about the damage to his truck. Although I was terribly shaken, I was not hurt! I did have whiplash for the next week or so, but if it hadn't been for my guardian angel, I would surely have died.

Tim feels that an angel saved his life, and as none of us was there with him, who are we to argue otherwise? In much the same way, who are we to disagree with Judith's account? Similar to Tim, Judith feels that there can be no other possible explanation for her miraculous escape from a road accident. What do you think?

Spinning Around

At about 6.30 am on a bright clear morning my husband was driving us both to work. Suddenly, my head jerked back as the car bumped like it had a punctured tyre. Then a second bump occurred and the car jerked into a concrete barrier. It hit on the left front side and turned around several times, whirling in a counter-clockwise fashion.

Fortunately, I had my seat belt on and so did my husband, so when we went into the turns I only scraped my forehead on the right side just at the hairline. I remember thinking, 'No, not again,' because of an accident we'd had a few years back on ice when the car span around in circles several times. We hadn't been wearing seat belts then and the accident had put us both in hospital for several days.

Anyway, when the car stopped shock turned to panic. We were facing the opposite direction and were looking into rush hour traffic coming straight at us. Incredibly, the cars were slowing down, separating and calmly going to either side of us like they were being directed by a traffic controller. No one had hit us as we span around and we hadn't hit anyone.

We got out and walked to the side of the road. A motorcycle rider stopped and called the police. The policemen that came to take us to hospital said that an angel must have been in the car with us giving us directions because there was no way anyone who wasn't a racing driver trained to cope in such situations could have walked away from the accident in one piece.

Later my husband told me that that a little voice came to him when we started spinning around and said, 'Let go of the wheel, everything is going to be fine.' He had listened to that voice and dropped his hands away from the wheel. He couldn't control the spin anyway. He said he looked at me and watched my head being bumped but he knew I would be fine.

Judith's account is dramatic but it is important to note that angel rescues can be just as spectacular in less immediate ways. Martin's story is gripping because it was only a few days after that the real miracle revealed itself.

Rescued by the Past

Even though my mum always told me not to go down to the train track I went down there one day with my dog, Lucky. I'd thrown his ball too hard and it had fallen onto the line. So I left our garden and climbed over the fence to get the ball. I was only seven but I wasn't afraid. I checked to see that there were no trains coming and carefully made my way over the track to reach the ball. Lucky didn't like going onto the track and stayed on the bank. I'm not sure if I slipped, everything happened so fast but I was lying down and couldn't move my ankle. A train was heading right towards me. I wasn't scared. It felt like I was watching someone else.

I'd been across the tracks before with my brothers. My mum would have gone crazy if she knew. The train got closer. I wasn't going to make it to safety in time. I can't remember how but the next thing I remember is being picked up from the track by an old man, moments before the train whirled past. He told me not to worry and I would be fine. My heart was pounding but I wasn't scared.

My mum came running out of the house. She must have seen us from the window. Instead of thanking the old man she screamed at him and said she would call the police if he didn't let me go. The man didn't say anything. He gently put me down, turned around and walked away. My mum yelled and screamed to him never to come back, saying if he had hurt me she would get them to put him in prison and throw away the key.

Hugging me and kissing me my mum bandaged my ankle and put me into bed. I felt so sleepy I couldn't say anything then, but when I woke up I told her that the man had saved me; he hadn't wanted to hurt me. I told her that I had been trying to get Lucky's ball and that I'd fallen over on the track. I begged her not to call the police.

My mum started to rock back wards and forwards in her chair. Then she got up and sat on the end of my bed. 'There's something I need to tell you. It's about your grand-father,' she said.

'But I don't have a grandfather,' I interrupted. 'You told me he was dead.'

'He isn't dead,' my mum replied. 'Before you were born I had a huge row with him. He didn't want me to marry your father and said if I did he didn't want to see me again. I begged and pleaded but he had made his mind up. I haven't seen him for eight years. He didn't even want to visit me when you were born. I didn't want to tell you all this because his lack of support hurt me so much.'

My mum stared at the floor, cleared her throat and continued. 'When I saw him carrying you today I lost it. I immediately thought he was trying to take you away from me but deep down I know he wouldn't ever hurt you. Then I thought he was trying to make amends for cutting me off but it's going to take a while for me to deal with my anger towards him. Perhaps in a couple of years I'll introduce you to him. Time is a healer.'

I started to cry. My mum held me and with comforting sighs and whispers told me that it wasn't my fault and I should not worry about anything.

A week later my mum got a phone call from her brother. When she put the receiver down her face had turned pale and she held onto the wall to stop herself losing her balance. My dad asked her if she was okay and she told him that her father had died a week ago in hospital. He'd died at the very same time that he had saved me from the train.

All these years later this story has been a source of tremendous strength and comfort to me. My mother recently passed away and my brother too, but neither of them were afraid of dying. I'm not afraid of dying either because I know that it's just like moving from one room to the next.

This next story was sent to me by a former colleague. The events she recalls happened to her ten years ago while she was on holiday in the USA. Samantha didn't hear voices or see strange lights but surely she was saved by an angel?

White Rabbit

I remember that the night was really dark, and bitterly cold. We had the heater on full blast in our car as we drove slowly along a rural mountain road in California. I drove very slowly because a fog had started to come down and I could hardly see in front of me.

I was looking for a motel. We had stopped to ask for directions at a gas station but my boyfriend at the time had clearly forgotten what he was told. Now we were just driving aimlessly in the hope that we might stumble upon the motel. I was cold. I was hungry. I was angry. It was impossible to know where we were heading in this fog.

My boyfriend suddenly remembered that we should take the third turning after a landmark we had recently passed so when we came to the third turning I headed off the main road onto what was a very rough road. The car bumped along the stones and it looked like we were heading into a field as we couldn't see any trees by the side of the road any more. I was convinced we had taken the wrong turning and swung the car around to head back. We drove for a few more minutes but didn't seem to find our way back to the main road. We should have reached it by now so we turned left instead in the hope that we would find a way out.

Suddenly, a white rabbit appeared in front of the car. I slammed on the brakes. I loved rabbits. When I was a little girl my pet rabbit, Samson, looked very much like this one. The rabbit's eyes fixed on us. My boyfriend cursed and told me turn out the headlights as it was clearly mesmerized by them. I turned them out but when I turned them on again the rabbit was still there. He didn't look frightened at all to me. I decided the only way to get him to move was to shoo him away.

I got out of the car and started to walk towards the rabbit. He didn't move. I stepped closer. He still didn't move. Eventually I got so close I could pet him. I've never seen such a brilliantly white rabbit before. The shine from his coat dazzled me. I leant down to pick him up and as I did my stomach lurched. I was standing on the edge of a cliff – no barrier, just a sheer drop off the edge of the mountain.

Gasping for air I stumbled backwards. I looked down and the rabbit had gone. There wasn't any sign of it. I shouted to my boyfriend to get out of the car. Within seconds he was by my side and could not believe his eyes either when he saw the sheer drop. We headed back to the car and sat in silence for a few minutes.

'Can you believe it?' I said to him, 'The rabbit just sat there when I walked towards him almost as if he wanted me to come close to the edge to see what was there.'

'What do you mean?' my boyfriend replied, raising his eyebrows. 'The rabbit made us stop but as soon as you got out of the car I saw it run away. Didn't you hear me yelling to you to come back inside the car? I just saw you wander off in a daze. I thought you were having a sulk because you were angry with me for messing up the directions and needed some time out.'

I don't know if the rabbit I saw was real or not but I'm convinced it was my guardian angel in disguise.

So you see, angels really can appear in the most unlikely disguises. If that rabbit hadn't jumped in front of their car it's almost certain that Samantha would have driven over the edge and been seriously injured or killed. The rabbit could have been real but why did Sam continue to see the rabbit when she got out of the car and her ex-boyfriend didn't? Perhaps Samantha's natural affinity with rabbits (remember, she adored her pet rabbit

Samson when she was little) was the medium the angels used to save her life?

Did Carolyn also see an angel when her life and the lives of her three children were in grave danger?

Off the Rails

A year ago I was driving my kids Charlotte, Christopher and Cain to school. As usual I was running late and feeling annoyed because Christopher had just announced that he had a swimming lesson that day but didn't have his swimming kit with him. I was really cross because I'd put his kit out ready with his school bag the night before. He was almost ten now and should be old enough to remember these things. I glanced at my watch. It was too late to turn back. He would simply have to miss swimming that day. With Christopher sulking and Charlotte and Cain busy reading their magazines the car fell silent. I welcomed the peace and started to think about a phone conference I needed to make as soon as I got into work.

The traffic slowed right down. There were road works ahead. It would take a good half hour before we got through the traffic lights. With nothing but queues ahead I decided to take a different route that was longer but would probably end up being quicker as there was less likelihood of traffic delays. There was a railroad ahead and I could see that other people were having the same idea so I indicated and started to turn around. But before I could complete my turn my engine suddenly cut out. I was stuck in the middle of the road across a train track, blocking both lanes, with cars beeping at me.

Over and over again I tried the ignition. The noise was unbearable as car horns sounded and brakes screamed all around me. People were trying to drive around me. I swore out loud – something I've never done before in front of the kids. Sensing my rising panic they started to get restless. The inside of the car steamed up. I was hot and sweaty and ready to burst into tears.

The face of a man appeared at my window. He had brown hair and was wearing a brown leather jacket with a white shirt underneath. It was hard to guess his age but I'd say he was about 50 or 60. I rolled down my window and he bent down to peer inside.

'This doesn't look good, does it?' he said calmly.

'You're telling me,' I said. 'The kids are late for school; I'm late for work and now I'm making everybody else late.'

'That's not what I meant to say,' the man replied, calmly. 'You need to move now because there's a train coming any minute. Get out of the car immediately and I'll give it a push.'

Within seconds I got my children and myself out of the car. My focus had been on getting the kids to school on time and getting to work on time but I had completely forgotten how dangerous a situation I was in. I mean, my engine had stalled in the middle of a train track! When I got out I could see the lights were flashing and the barriers were ready to go down. People were waiting on the station.

I rushed with my kids under the barriers. As I was running away I saw the man give my car a little push and it rolled safely to the other side just as the barrier closed behind it. I saw him leap over the barriers and get into a purple car and then the train soared past. I realized that the train was coming into the station at a considerable speed and it would never have been able to avoid hitting and killing us.

After the train had gone past I was keen to thank the man who had saved our lives. I strained my eyes looking for the purple car but where was it? The train had only obscured my view for a few moments. How could he have vanished like that?

By now a few other people had stopped to ask if I needed help. My car was still blocking the road, after all. It took four or five of them to push it onto the pavement. The strangest thing of all is that all the people who helped me kept saying what a miracle it was my car hadn't stalled on the tracks. For them it had stalled just after the barriers. I know that it had stalled in the middle of the track. My kids knew it too. They remembered the man helping us and unfortunately they remembered me swearing too.

My kids got to school late that day and I missed my phone conference. It really didn't matter though. I don't get stressed about things like that any more. I've got my priorities right. The angel in the brown jacket helped me understand what really matters.

Ed's incredible reprieve is similar to Carolyn's in that, whether human or divine, his celestial rescue is miraculous. I've left his story in his own words.

Keys to the Garage

In 1977 I left school and began a four-year-long apprenticeship as a car mechanic. Ever since I could remember I'd been crazy about cars and trucks and getting the opportunity to train and earn money at the same time as doing something I loved seemed like heaven. I'd never really felt I belonged at school but now I felt right for the first time in my life.

The guys at the garage really took me under their wing and after a year or so they started to trust me to do minor repair jobs. Eager to learn as much as I could I ran headlong towards every challenge. I was so keen that I probably took on too much too soon and to catch up I'd often be the last one to leave the garage and lock up at night.

One evening, instead of going home after I'd finished my jobs for the day, I decided to work in advance on a job that was due to be completed the next day. It was Saturday tomorrow and the guys would really appreciate closing early for the weekend.

So I drove the Mini scheduled for repair work into the garage. I attached the hoist onto the front bumper and raised it up just far enough for me to crawl underneath. Immediately, I could see a problem with the suspension. I was just about to crawl out and grab some bolts when the hoist suddenly came down. I was trapped underneath. I pushed upwards as hard as I could but it was impossible. Working alone I hadn't had the safety net of someone checking constantly that the safety lock was in place. I cursed my stupidity and my eagerness to please. It was slowly crushing me to death.

I called out for someone to help me. I only heard my voice echoing around the garage. It was close to nine o'clock on a Friday night. Nobody was going to hear me and besides, the garage door had a self-locking mechanism once someone was inside. That's why there was a big sign next to the door saying that two people were to be in the garage at all times. All I could think as the car gradually crushed the life out of me was that I deserved to die. I had thought myself above rules and regulations.

All at once I heard footsteps. I screamed at whoever it was to help me and pull the lever to lift the car off. I heard the lever move. In one last frantic effort I strained my arms to push the car away. I rolled over as quickly as I could.

For a minute or two I was in so much pain that all I could do was roll around in agony. Eventually the pain eased and I looked around for the man who had saved my life. He wasn't there. I called out. No one answered. I looked towards the garage doors. They were still locked. Where had the man gone and why had he vanished so mysteriously?

It took a while for me to stagger towards the garage door and after fumbling with the lock clumsily with blooded hands I opened the door. I took a deep breath as I stepped outside. The pain in my chest had eased but I'd be bruised for a long time, not just physically but emotionally.

I went to the office next door to the garage and phoned my workmates to tell them what had happened. They sent an ambulance over right away. Later at the hospital my boss reminded me that I belonged to a team. He knew that my intentions had been good but it wasn't right for me to make decisions for the team without clearing it with them first. I understood what he was saying. I'd learned a powerful lesson that night. As my boss was leaving I asked him to thank whoever it was that had come to help me. My boss looked puzzled and said there hadn't been anyone there. All the team had been either at the pub that evening or at home with their families and no one else had keys to the garage.

At the time I didn't fully understand what had happened to me that night. When I told my mother about it she said that the mystery person who pulled the lever could have been an angel. Whoever he or she was – human or divine – I know that I'm alive today because someone or something heard my screams and saved my life.

Clearly angels can save people's lives in many different ways, but all the accounts so far have been personal involving very few people. Can angels help larger groups of people? This next account is outstanding because it was witnessed by dozens of people. Lisa was 17 years old at the time. Here's her story.

The Ferris Wheel

We'd all looked forward to this trip for weeks. We'd just finished our mock exams and were in the mood for fun. Six of my best friends met at my house and we all got the bus together to an amusement park near our village.

It was a warm summer day. When we arrived it was great to hear all the screaming and laughter you'd expect at an amusement park. It was really busy and there were major queues for almost all the attractions. I didn't mind. It was just great to soak up the atmosphere of the place and smell that popcorn.

Although we'd only done two rides each by lunchtime we were all having a brilliant time. We decided to queue up for an old favourite; the Ferris wheel – although this Ferris wheel was possibly the biggest I have ever seen. I remember feeling a bit nervous as I've never liked heights but, of course, not showing it. We whiled away the time chatting and people-spotting and after about 20 minutes we finally got to the front of the queue.

We got onto the Ferris wheel and it started to turn slowly around. Then suddenly it jerked to a halt. I looked down. Everybody was screaming. The guy in the control box was slumped over the controls. People were trying to pull open the door but it was locked from the inside. His body weight must have pushed a lever because the Ferris wheel started to move again but it was going very fast. I clutched onto the safety bar and gritted my teeth. My friend was close to vomiting beside me. At this speed something terrible was going to happen. With the wind pushing against my face I looked down again at the control box. There was somebody inside. He was lifting the man away from the control box and adjusting the controls. The Ferris wheel slowed to a steady pace and within minutes we were safely on the ground.

When we got to the ground an emergency team arrived. Curiously, they couldn't get inside the control box; it was still locked from the inside. They kicked open the door and took the man out on a stretcher. There wasn't anyone else inside. I asked my friends on the wheel and other people if they had seen the guy too and they all nodded. People waiting in the queue for their turn had also seen him but nobody knew who he was. He wasn't in the control box when the door was opened. Twenty years later and I'm still mystified.

A number of people on the Ferris wheel that day were convinced that an angel saved their lives. Lisa is not completely sure but wonders what other possible explanation there could be. In much the same way, Catherine can't find any other explanation for her son's narrow escape.

Somebody Called Samuel

About ten o'clock one morning in August I decided to take my kids to get some fresh air in a small park that was just a few blocks away from where we lived. We had only moved to the area a few days before and my kids had spent most of that stuck in the house as I unpacked box after box after box. The house was in chaos and I had so much to do but as it was such a beautiful day I though we'd all feel better getting some fresh air and sunshine.

'I'm too old for parks,' my eldest, Samuel, screamed down at me from the top of the stairs. 'I'm twelve not three.'

'Parks are boring,' echoed Sally, my seven-going-on-seventeen-year-old daughter.

'Okay,' I said, 'We don't have to go into the park. We can just walk around it. You need some fresh air, guys, and besides there might be some great shops to check out on the other side of the park.'

Within moments Sam and Sally had their shoes on, ready to do what they loved best these days – shopping. I sighed and grabbed my jacket, hoping that my kids were just going through a materialistic phase. Then we all left the house and headed off in the direction of the park.

It was warmer than I thought when we got outside and before long I wasn't just carrying my jacket I was carrying the kid's jumpers as well. I toyed with the idea of dropping the jackets off back home but dismissed it as it hadn't been easy getting the kids out of the house the first time. As we walked I asked them how they felt about starting new schools. I tried to reassure them that it was understandable that they would be nervous and that the first few weeks would be hard, but once they settled in they would be fine.

'I don't like it here,' interrupted Sam. 'Why couldn't I stay at my old school?'

'Yeah, mum,' echoed Sally. 'You're so selfish for taking us away from our friends and from dad. He's the best dad ever.'

My eyes filled with tears. My kids knew that things hadn't been right between me and their dad, Roger, for a while. What they didn't know – because I didn't have the heart to tell them – was that their dad had had an affair with one of his students at the university where he was a senior lecturer. She was only 18. The affair had been going on for two months before I found out. At first I hoped it would just be a casual fling but a year after promising to stop seeing her he still was. When he came up with the crazy idea of us both seeing other people but staying married for the children, I snapped. I had to get out and start somewhere new. Roger knew where we were and I told him that he could visit the kids any time he liked but there hadn't been a phone call or a visit yet.

'Yeah,' said Sam. 'Why couldn't we stay with dad and not with you?'

At that moment I hated my kids. This was hard for me too. They didn't want me. They wanted their reckless dad. I was the enemy.

'Here,' I said, handing Sam my mobile. 'Give your dad a call and ask him if you can live with him.'

We were approaching the park now and Sam grabbed my mobile and began to dial. I sat down on a bench and watched him walk around the park as he talked. Sally was sitting on a swing nearby, ignoring me. I closed my eyes and swallowed hard. This was one of the toughest and most painful days of my life. I loved my kids and everything I was doing was for them but they didn't seem to feel my love.

While I was sitting there I heard a voice calling, 'Samuel!' That's all the voice said. I thought it was odd because nobody called my son Samuel except my mother. He had announced when he was nine that he hated being called Samuel and would only answer to Sam.

It sounded like a young man's voice. It was the calmest and friendliest voice I have ever heard. I looked behind me to see if anyone was calling out to my son from the road. There was only traffic rushing past.

Sam was still talking on his mobile and did not seem to have heard the voice. Perhaps it was my imagination? Perhaps it was the sound of the traffic or someone in a passing car? But the voice had come from my right side as if someone was close at hand.

Again I heard the voice. Puzzled, I stood up and asked Sally if she heard anything. She shook her head and sighed as she always seemed to do when I asked her something these days.

Then I saw Sam stop walking and take the mobile away from his ear. He looked around him. Had he heard the voice too? A split second later a tree crashed down a few feet ahead of him. It rested across the path with its branches scattered everywhere. It fell where Sam would have walked if he had not stopped at the moment I heard the voice again. Shocked and bewildered I ran towards Sam, closely followed by a frightened Sally. Sam, in his usual cool manner, looked at the tree and at me, then put the mobile phone back to his ear and told his dad that he had to go.

'Mum, who called my name?' he asked. 'You know I hate it when people call me Samuel.'

'I heard it too. I don't know who called out. There's nobody here.'

'Well then,' said Sally with great excitement in your voice. 'It had to be your guardian angel, Sam.'

Sam started to cry. Instinctively I reached out and held him and for once he didn't push me away. 'Dad's not interested in seeing us, is he? What did I do wrong?' he sobbed.

I stroked my son's hair and told him that he had done absolutely nothing wrong and that he was special and much loved, whatever his father said or did.

'You're just saying that,' he replied.

'I'm not. What more proof do you need? Your guardian angel saved your life today.'

Sam looked at me and his eyes brightened. Sally wrestled her way in between us and told us that just because an angel had saved Sam today it didn't mean that he was any more special than her. After such high emotion and tension all the three of us could do was laugh.

After that remarkable day life got easier for us all. The kids found ways to show their love and respect and I found ways to communicate better with them. It's not been easy since the divorce, but whoever said life was meant to be easy?

Catherine doesn't know if the voice she heard was real or imagined but as she was new to the area it's unlikely anyone would know her son's name. Human or divine, she is convinced that a guardian angel was watching over her and her children that day.

Kim also heard a voice that she believes saved her life.

Ringing in My Ear

A couple of years ago I had the most incredible experience. If anybody else told me it had happened to them I don't think I'd have believed them. But it was real and it did happen to me.

It was about 9 pm and I was driving home from work. I don't normally work that late but on this occasion I had to. Tim and Lisa, two of my colleagues, were in the car with me. They usually caught the train back but there were huge problems on South West Trains that day so I offered to give them a lift. We were all feeling pretty tired so we didn't talk much.

About 20 minutes into the journey I heard this high-pitched sound ringing in my ear. It got so distracting that if it didn't stop soon I'd have to pull over and stop the car. We'd left the motorway now and were on a windy road into town. The ringing was getting louder and louder so I pulled to the side of the road. As soon as I did the ringing stopped. Delighted, I turned on the engine again and started to edge forward but as soon as I did the ringing was back. It was unbearable.

Tim and Lisa were getting concerned and asked me what the problem was and before I could answer a speeding car hurtled past us. It was driving on the wrong side of the road. Cars on the other side hooted their horns loudly. If I hadn't stopped there would have been nowhere for my car to go but to plough into either the speeding car or the oncoming traffic on the other side of the road. It would have been a head-on collision.

Moments later we heard police sirens and they flashed past in hot pursuit. I don't know if the driver was drunk, speeding because the car had been stolen or if the brakes had failed, but without that ringing in my ear I wouldn't be alive today and neither would Tim or Lisa. There was a guardian angel with us that day.

Some people believe that a ringing sound in the ear – that we all hear occasionally – is an angel talking to us or, if you prefer, a heavenly download. Angels transfer information, guidance and assistance to us this way and it sounds a bit like a computer modem connecting with the internet. I don't mean tinnitus or the harsh, grinding noise you get from serious ear infections (if the sound becomes too loud, painful and intrusive seek advice from your doctor) I mean a gentle high-pitched sound that lasts for a few moments and then fades away.

On some occasions the ringing is accompanied by a throbbing sensation on the earlobe. You don't need to understand the information recorded in the message consciously – you just need to be open to receiving it. The information will be stored in your unconscious where it will have a positive influence on your thoughts and your actions. The next time you hear it, instead of rubbing your ears roughly, why not relax and let the angels speak to you? Stop what you are doing for a moment and let the wisdom sink in.

Back to Kim's story: was the voice her sixth sense or intuition, or was it the voice of an angel? Researchers now believe that everyone is born with a sixth sense but we have simply forgotten how to use it in this age of technology. Intuition or the voice of an angel? The more I read such stories the more I question if there is really any difference between the two.

Zac's story comes next and it sits well with Kim's as he also got a warning while he was driving. Like Kim, he is convinced that his life was saved by an angel.

Put Your Foot Down

Back in the mid-eighties I was a policeman. During one of my routine patrols, I was driving through a residential but hilly area. As my car was climbing a steep hill one day

I sensed a presence in the passenger seat next to me. There was nothing there, of course.

When I got to the top of the hill I heard a loud voice telling me to 'Brake'. It sounded exactly like the voice of the first officer I'd been paired up with years ago; calm but assertive. He'd died about ten years before in a car accident which upset me greatly because he'd always been such a cautious driver, even when the sirens were flashing. He had told me many a time to slow down or brake so at first I thought I was just remembering.

I heard the voice again and then again. I shrugged my shoulders to make sure I wasn't getting sleepy. Nope. I was wide awake. I heard the voice for what must have been the tenth time and so not really knowing why, I made a half-hearted attempt to brake even though I wasn't over the speed limit.

Suddenly, I felt a bolt of energy through my body and the next instant my foot left the floor and slammed on the brakes. I wasn't moving my feet; something else was. I also felt myself pulling the steering wheel to the right (again without doing this myself). At this time, I was now about three quarters of the way up the next hill. A van came over the top of the hill (heading directly towards me) driving erratically.

The van swerved to the left and narrowly missed me. I hit my emergency lights and siren and as I did I saw a dead animal – it looked like a deer – lying in the other lane. I turned my car around and saw the van waiting at the side of the road.

I didn't get out of my car. I just rolled down my window and looked at the driver. He looked terrified as I'm sure I did. I told him that if that happened again he should hit the dead animal instead of swerving as he did. I told him we could both have been killed. He nodded and I phoned for assistance to clear the dead animal from the road.

Whether you believe in angels or not I suggest that if anyone hears a voice speaking calmly and clearly to them, they listen.

In this next story contributed by Grace, a young mother of two, both a voice and a gentle pair of hands make a surprising appearance.

The Midwife

Ever since I can remember I have wanted to become a mother, so when I got pregnant unexpectedly at the age of 20 I was thrilled. My family and boyfriend, however, didn't share my joy. My boyfriend said he wasn't ready to be a dad and my mum wanted me to finish my degree first. I understood their concern but an abortion was out of the question. I knew it would be hard raising my baby alone but I would find a way to cope. I wanted this baby more than I have ever wanted anything in my life.

Seeing that I wasn't going to change my mind my mum and my boyfriend slowly came around to the idea. My sister, who was 14 at the time, was freaked out by the whole thing. As my bump got bigger and bigger and my trousers tighter she'd often screw up her face in disgust. One day she came into my room and asked me if I was frightened of giving birth. She told me that her friends had said it would be really painful and labour could last days. I hadn't really experienced much pain in my life and I was scared but I wasn't going to admit that to my sister.

As the months passed and my due date grew closer and closer I started to get mild panic attacks. I'd have terrible dreams about being torn apart when I was giving birth or giving birth to a monster. I'd wake up in a sweat, shaking all over. I couldn't tell anyone. It had been so hard to convince them that this was what I wanted, how could I turn round now and say I was frightened, not of having a baby but of giving birth? I had to stay strong.

On 17 September at 9.30 pm I was sitting on the sofa reading a magazine when I felt dampness under my legs. I'd read every pregnancy book I could lay my hands on so I knew this was it. My baby was getting ready to arrive. I called my mum and half an hour later we were at the hospital.

When I arrived at the hospital a nurse examined me and told me that although my waters had broken it would be some time before the real labour began. I should, however, stay the night and get some sleep to prepare myself for the big day tomorrow. I remember looking at the clock and it was close to midnight.

It made sense for my boyfriend and mum to head home and get some sleep so after saying goodnight to them both I hobbled into my cubicle, got changed, brushed my teeth and went to bed. A nurse came to ask me if I was okay and when I nodded she drew the privacy curtains around me.

I must have dozed off for an hour or two because when I woke up the clock said 2.33 am. Abruptly, I felt this blinding pain. It ripped right through me. I had never hurt so much in my entire life. I grabbed the handrails and pressed the buzzer on the wall for help. I started to breathe very quickly, my heart was racing. I was having a panic attack.

I swung my legs over the side in an attempt to cool down and start some deep breathing to control the pain and as I did I felt a hand brush past my cheek. I looked up and saw a nurse with black hair and pale skin brushing my hair behind my ears. She had the sweetest, kindest, melting eyes.

'I don't know what to do,' I gasped. 'I don't think I can get through this. It isn't anything like the books say.'

'There is no need to be afraid. Your family is on its way,' she said reassuringly. 'What I need you to do is breathe deeply and trust me.'

The woman hummed gently to herself and started to rub my head. It felt blissful. Her hands were like soft velvet. After a few moments she asked me to open my eyes. 'You're already fully dilated. Your baby is coming. The nurse and doctor will arrive in a minute to deliver your baby. All you need to do is to keep breathing. Copy me.'

I started to breathe as she said and once I got the hang of it I closed my eyes. Instantly, I felt calmer and more in control. I opened my eyes and the nurse had gone. I wasn't afraid. She'd told me that help was on its way. I just kept breathing deeply and steadily until I could feel that my baby was ready for the final push. Then I rang again for the nurse.

The same nurse who had examined me earlier arrived. I told her that the baby was already coming. She didn't believe me and told me I probably needed to use the toilet. I asked her to make sure and after she checked me she left immediately to get a doctor. My baby was definitely on its way.

Moments later my mum and boyfriend arrived. Both of them held my hands as I was wheeled into the delivery room. The doctor confirmed that I was fully dilated. He asked me when my contractions had started and I said I'd only had a couple of contractions at about 2.30 am. I don't think he believed me because I wasn't sweating or screaming and it was now a few minutes past seven in the morning and he asked the nurse what painkillers she had given me. He raised his eyebrows when the nurse said I hadn't been given any.

'I guess you're just a natural at this then,' he said reassuringly, and five or so pushes and ten minutes later my little girl was born. As she lay on my chest I savoured this incredible moment. I didn't have wings but I felt as if I was flying.

Later that afternoon I asked my mum when she had got her call and she said that a woman had called her at about midnight to tell her that I was sleeping and that it would be best to make sure she was there by seven o'clock the next morning.

I wanted to thank the sweet nurse who had helped make my delivery so peaceful and show her my newborn but when I asked, none of the other nurses knew who she was. They said there wasn't anyone on duty that night with jet black hair. I asked them to check both part-time and full-time staff but nobody could tell who she was. I asked them who had called my mum and boyfriend in the night to tell them to come in and nobody could tell me who that was either.

It's been a couple of years since my first delivery. I'm now married to my boyfriend and have had another baby since then. The second birth wasn't quite as pain free, but as I'd been through it all before I wasn't as anxious and stayed calm. I often wonder who that amazing nurse with the sweet voice was. Whoever she was I feel blessed beyond words by her gentle touch.

Grace's story isn't strictly an 'angel saved my life' scenario as at no time during her delivery was her life in danger. It is, however, included here as it is still a kind of celestial rescue. Grace was terrified and uncertain about giving birth for the first time and from the depth of their love the angels helped give her a joyous, pain-free experience that filled her with awe and gratitude.

Why Me?

One of the hardest things to reconcile when it comes to celestial rescue stories is why some people are given comfort or warning in times of need and danger and others are not. After reading and hearing countless stories where people found themselves narrowly escaping tragedy, my inclination is that angels can't always prevent terrible things happening – an accident, illness or sudden death – but what they can sometimes do is adjust or change your part in it. The crash will happen but you won't be killed.

But why are some people saved and others not? Did they not heed the warnings? Or are the reasons why some of us must live and some of us must die simply beyond our grasp? Such questions are unanswerable but what we do know is that for those who do survive, the message that their time on earth is not yet over is both miraculous and deeply humbling. It is also a poignant reminder of how precious our time on earth is.

The stories of those who have survived or narrowly escaped natural disasters, accidents or terrorist attacks bear powerful witness to just how humbling a last-minute reprieve can be. Sometimes this reprieve comes in the form of a premonition. People from all over the world have reported surprising dreams, visions and premonitions that warned them of impending tragedy. There are even rumours circulating on the net that Bin Laden was so concerned about premonitions like these that he was worried they would give away the 9/11 plot.

Just as remarkable as the stories of people who believe the angels warned them are the stories of people who would have definitely been caught up in a tragedy if it weren't for sudden changes of plan or unexpected events on the day it occurred. Was some unforeseen force guiding their lives that day? Clare's story is fascinating because she experienced both a premonition and a last-minute change of plan on the morning of 7 July, 2005, when four coordinated terrorist bombings hit the London transport system, killing 52 innocent people and injuring hundreds.

Kicking and Screaming

Most weekday mornings I catch the tube into King's Cross and get to my office a few minutes' walk away by 9 am. The night before the attack I had the strangest dream. I was in a tube train and suddenly everything went black and quiet. I was completely alone and then I heard a voice telling me to work from home the next day.

When I woke up the dream lingered in my mind. I normally work from home on Fridays. Today was Thursday and I saw no need to change anything this week. I got out of bed and dressed as normal. Then I went into the nursery to wake up my little boy. I spent a few moments looking at him while he slept and then gently lifted him out of his cot.

At 7.30 am my son's nanny phoned in to say she wasn't feeling very well. She told me not to worry though as her flatmate – who was also a nanny – could look after George for a day or so while she got better.

Half an hour later I opened the door to a nervous-looking young girl called Alex. I gave her a five-minute tour of the house and then told her to phone me at work so I could run through George's schedule for the day with her. I didn't feel very comfortable leaving George with a complete stranger but I'd only been back at work for five weeks since he'd been born. I toyed with the idea of working from home but Alex seemed friendly enough and she was already loading the dishwasher and tidying up — without even being asked. It was about 8.20 now and I picked George up from his highchair and handed him carefully to Alex.

George wasn't happy. He started to scream and kick as soon as I placed him in Alex's arms. Alex did her best to try and soothe him but George was having none of it. After a few minutes Alex suggested that I leave because seeing me probably made the transition worse for him. Feeling hot and tense I grabbed my briefcase and went outside. I could hear Alex screaming from outside the house. I could still hear him as I walked up the road to the tube station. I could still hear him as I went into the tube station.

I was just about to pass my ticket through the barriers when the phone rang. It was Alex. I could hear George still screaming in the background. She said she thought George was coming down with something and wanted to take him to the doctor. I couldn't bear it any longer. I phoned work to say I'd be working from home that day and headed back. I'd take George to the doctor.

I couldn't hear George screaming when I put the key in the door. Frantic with worry I ran into the kitchen. They weren't there. I went into the lounge and still no sign of them. I called out their names but still no reply. I rushed upstairs and when I got to the top I heard muffled noises coming from the playroom. I opened the door and there was Alex with George babbling happily in her arms. The radio was on and Alex was singing songs to him. Alex told me that as soon as she had turned the radio on George had calmed down. She apologized for phoning me and suggested I head back to work.

Work – after the morning I'd had! I sank down into a chair and thanked Alex for her help but told her I'd take over from here. To be honest, seeing George so content with Alex had made me a little jealous.

One hour later I turned the television on and heard the horrendous news. For me, and I'm sure for others like me who could well have been on one of those buses or tube trains, the tragedy transformed my perspective on life. I'm deeply humbled; grateful for every precious moment and for the miracle of my son's kicking and screaming signalling that my time on earth is not yet finished.

It's incredible isn't it? Once your life has been touched by an angel even a child kicking and screaming can be a sign from them! Clare's story can easily be explained as a series of events that upset her schedule for the day and understandable separation anxiety on the part of her son. But you'd have a struggle convincing Clare that her dream and her son crying were anything other than a warning from her guardian angel.

Someone Is Watching Over Us

Celestial rescues are not confined to any particular spot in the world. I've gathered angel stories from all over the globe showing that there is a universal attraction to the idea that 'someone is watching over us'. These stories prove that a growing number of people believe in angels who have a greater power than us and who can rescue us from danger. And the more people who believe the more likely it is for angelic intervention to occur in our daily lives.

According to the Mayan calendar, the year 2012 will be a year of overwhelming change in the world population. This isn't the place to debate the astrological significance of 2012 but there is no doubt that the number of people who are spiritually aware is growing steadily. Even though wars continue to tear lives apart, there are still people who can transcend religious, ethnic and cultural differences to see the oneness of all humankind and by so doing bring love and hope into violence and conflict.

All over the world people are opening their hearts to angels and every astonishing angel story that spreads the word is a celestial rescue in itself, because it reminds us that the world is full of astonishing and uplifting experiences. The more we focus on what is uplifting and light hearted in our lives the closer the angels will draw to us and the more miraculous our lives and our world will become.

Naturally, it helps if you have had an angel experience of your own but even if you haven't, reading the stories of other people will help open your heart and mind to unexplained possibilities. Perhaps the angels have already been dipping into your life and you've been too busy or too preoccupied to notice?

Although I've had a few experiences of my own, many of the stories I read still leave me wondering if the events were real, a coincidence or only real in the mind of the narrator. In each case I find myself coming to the same conclusion – if an experience causes any of us to wonder if angels or a higher power are watching over us and guiding our lives in some way, it is a celestial rescue or, as others like to call it, a miracle.

CHAPTER 5

Carried by an Angel

The angels ... regard our safety, undertake our
defence, direct our ways and exercise a constant
solicitude that no evil befalls us.

John Calvin

If you thought the stories in the previous chapter were
astonishing, read on because the ones in this chapter are
truly out of this world. We'll plunge right in with Trudy's
account: a dramatic example of an angel story which
appears beyond belief. Did an angel save Trudy's brother
or did he somehow find within himself the strength and
courage to survive? Sometimes it is hard to tell the
difference because both are miracles, but Trudy knows
what her heart believes.

Fly Like the Wind

When I got up that morning the first thing I did was look out of my window. I was hoping to have fresh turf laid down in my garden today. The old turf had been removed last week but because it had been raining solidly for the last four days the gardeners had delayed putting down the new turf. There was mud everywhere but with clear blue skies and the sun shining I was hopeful that work on the garden would resume.

I put on my dressing gown and slippers and went downstairs to make a cup of tea. While I was making my tea I felt a breeze lift the hair from my forehead. Perhaps I had left a door or a window open? I went to check and as I did I dropped my mug of tea. My brother was standing in the garden with bloody marks on his face.

I ran outside and put his arm around my shoulder to help him inside. It took a while as he could barely walk but eventually we got inside. Then I sat him on a chair and called for an ambulance. My brother was clearly dazed but he grabbed my arm and begged me to listen.

He told me that he had been flying and then he startled to ramble about his motorcycle. I didn't really listen but when the paramedics arrived he became more lucid. He told us he had been walking home and a speeding car had hit him. The driver hadn't stopped and he'd been left bleeding and bruised by the roadside. Then he told me he saw a pair of arms in the air, reaching out to him. The arms lifted him up and he had a sensation of flying through the air. The next thing he could remember was standing at my doorstep.

At the time I wasn't paying much attention to what he was saying, but later when I got home I went into the garden and noticed that the only footsteps in the mud were mine and those belonging to my brother. I was in for an even greater shock a week later when the police told me that my brother's hit and run had taken place over ten miles away. There was no way he could have arrived at my house by himself. Somebody helped him and the only explanation I can think of is that it was an angel.

Trudy also believes that the breeze she felt lifting her hair was the breath of an angel trying to get her attention so that she would discover her brother in the garden. Being physically lifted to safety by an angel, as Trudy's brother was, is incredible but it isn't as uncommon an experience as you might think. I've collected numerous stories from people who report the sensation of floating or flying away from danger.

I've not had the sensation of flying when I'm conscious, but in my dreams I'm a high flier. It took a while to master the technique but now I can duck and dive and even somersault. It's downhill all the way when I wake up! Seriously, though, if you've ever flown in your dreams you'll have some idea of how liberating and, forgive the pun, uplifting the sensation can be if it happens when you are awake. Donna's story is another astonishing example.

Over the Hill

There is nothing that gives me greater pleasure than walking in the countryside, so when the opportunity came up to stay with Mary, an old school friend, in the Lake District I couldn't refuse. Like me, Mary was an enthusiastic walker and I was very excited about visiting a place I'd heard so much about.

The scenery was breathtaking as the train drew into Windermere and I couldn't wait to put on my walking boots. The first few days of my trip Mary accompanied me but I soon noticed that she didn't share my enthusiasm for ever longer and more challenging walks.

'You're nearly 50, Donna,' she said to me one day as we came back from a three-hour trek. 'Isn't it time you slowed down a bit?'

'Me slow down? I don't know how to.'

It was no surprise to me the next morning when Donna opted to stay at home. I asked her if she was okay and she told me that last year she had been diagnosed with high blood pressure and although exercise was really good for her she couldn't afford to overdo it. Now

I understood why she had wanted to sit down a lot more than I was used to on our walks. I was cross with her for not telling me she wasn't as fit as she used to be and suggested that we spend the day shopping and going on a river tour instead. But she knew how much I wanted to go walking and told me not to worry, she would be fine. She said it made her happy to see me happy.

Walking with others is a joyful experience but walking alone has its merits too. Over the years I've found that it can almost be a form of meditation for me, and what better place to walk alone and soak in the rich beauty of nature than the Lake District; so often described as heaven on earth?

The first few hours of my solo walk were blissful but after stopping for lunch I started to lose my bearings. With dusk fast approaching I realized that I had to get off the mountain. Once darkness fell it would be impossible to see where I was going. I started to make my way downhill. I had seen a group of cottages in the distance that looked vaguely familiar and even if one of the cottages didn't belong to Mary at least I could ask for help and directions and quite possibly a taxi there.

Navigating my way down the mountain was considerably harder than I thought. Soon I was dangerously sliding down rocks and cutting my ankles with stones. The light was fading fast and I was terrified that I'd lose my footing. I was also feeling very tired and the distinct possibility of not making it down the mountain in time flashed through my mind. Would Mary send out a search party? Would anyone find me or would I fall, injure myself and freeze overnight? It was a nightmare.

I strained my eyes to look at my watch. It was nearly 7 pm and within half an hour it would be pitch black. There was such a long way for me to go to reach lights and safety and I was getting weaker and weaker. I was really frightened and instead of trying to inch further down the mountain I sat down and cried. I thought about my life and all the people I loved. I thought about my husband waiting patiently for me at home. I thought about Mary and what a wonderful friend she'd been over the years. I thought about all the things I wanted to say and do. I might never get the chance now.

My hands were really freezing now; I hadn't even worn gloves as it had been fairly warm when I set off in the morning. I tucked them in my coat and made one last effort to stand and make my way down. I wasn't going to sit here and die. I was going to fight for the life I loved. I prayed to find the strength to make my way safely home. Then I slipped but instead of falling I felt as if I was floating down the side of the mountain. I heard what sounded like a choir of children singing. What was happening to me? Was I dying?

No. I was at the bottom on the mountain looking at Mary's cottage a few hundred yards away. I had made it.

But how was it possible? I blinked and rubbed my eyes. My hands were warm. I looked at my watch. It was half past seven and yet it didn't feel as if half an hour had passed since I last checked my watch. There was no way in my weakened state that I could have got down the mountain in half an hour. And yet, here I was safely back and feeling energized.

I walked to Mary's cottage and rang the doorbell. She told me that she was starting to get worried but in her heart of hearts she knew I would be fine. I didn't tell her about my experience. I sensed that something strange had happened to me but I was scared to admit it to myself. I've gone over and over what happened that evening in my mind since. It's possible that I somehow slipped down the side of my mountain and landed on my feet but unlikely because my coat didn't have any mud stains on it and I didn't have any bruises on my body.

The only conclusion I come to time and time again is that my guardian angel carried me to safety. Perhaps when I asked for the strength and courage to face a difficult situation I tapped into an invisible power and grace. Perhaps if I hadn't asked for help my angel wouldn't have been able to help me. But I did ask and I owe my life to the angels who lifted me up with their heavenly song.

Nobody actually saw an angel in the two lifting stories above but in this next story Jonathon believes he met one. Did he meet a genuine angel or another person guided by an angel? It's often very hard to distinguish between the two but Jonathon is convinced that an angel tapped him on the shoulder.

Follow Me

I was 21, fresh out of college and eager to spend a year travelling around the States before I went back home to Switzerland to begin my apprenticeship at my dad's law firm. I didn't realize or appreciate it at the time but I was incredibly lucky. Not only did I have a job lined up but my parents were financing my gap year.

My dad had warned me to avoid travelling at night, and in the cities to stay away from dangerous areas. With all the confidence of youth and convinced of my own immortality I ignored that advice to my peril.

A month into my trip and I was savouring the New York experience. I loved the buzz of the place and made a mental note to myself to return and possibly live there one day. I spent most of the first day sightseeing and wandering the streets, really soaking up the atmosphere of the place. Having seen New York in so many films I felt like I knew it already. If I had taken the trouble to buy a street guide I would perhaps have figured out that only a few streets divide areas that are safe from areas that are deadly dangerous.

If I had acquainted myself with the area I would have been aware that my decision to get on a street heading west in the early evening was unwise. Within a matter of moments I was surrounded by a group of men or perhaps boys. They were wearing hoods and it was clear that if I didn't hand over my bag they'd take it by force. They were brandishing knives. Shaking and sweating with fear I started to take my bag off my shoulder but before I could hand it to them they had disappeared. Someone tapped on my shoulder. I looked around and I saw a policeman. You have no idea how glad I was to see him.

'What are you doing here?' he asked. 'You shouldn't be wandering around here at this time of night. Tourists are easy pickings and even if you'd given them your money they still might have killed you.'

I realized then how naïve and stupid I had been. He seemed to sense how I was feeling and said, 'Follow me, I know a safe place where you can stay tonight.' Then he started walking and in about three or four minutes we were outside a hotel.

Not sure what to do or how to thank him properly I reached for my wallet to tip him. The policeman laughed and said, 'Cops can't take tips.'

'But how can I repay you?'

'Make the world a safer place,' he replied. 'And you can start by putting that wallet away. Flashing it around like that is inviting a mugging.'

I turned my gaze to my wallet and put it back in my bag and when I looked up he was gone. I looked down a side street where he might have turned but there was no one anywhere. I looked up and down the street I was standing in but couldn't see him either – he had vanished.

At the hotel I got a comfortable room and had something to eat. There was a New York guide there and still a bit shaky from my experience I lay down on my bed and started to study it. Within a day or so I had become better acquainted with the streets of New York. I realized that it would have taken hours to walk from the dangerous area I had been in to the hotel I was staying in. That policeman must have been an angel. He had transported me almost instantly from one part of the city to another and then he had vanished. I didn't pick up on it then but the policeman had also spoken to me in my native French, which was very unusual.

I took a few more months to travel the States and when my money ran out I headed back home. My father was furious when I told him that I didn't want to work in his firm. I wanted to become a police officer. I wanted to help make the world a safer place and to protect other people from danger in the same way I'd been saved.

My guardian angel did more than save my life that day; he gave me a sense of purpose. I didn't know who

I was before or what I was meant to be doing with my life. Fifteen years later and I've never regretted my decision to join the force. My life was saved and I've now made it my business to save the lives of others.

Jonathon truly believes that he saw and spoke to an angel and that this angel changed the direction of his life. The following story is another example of angelic intervention changing the course of a person's life forever. The intervention came primarily in the form of voices rather than through sensation or vision as was the case with Jonathon, but in this instance Glenda recognized that the angelic voice was her own.

Stop and Change Direction

About five years ago I had a mind-blowing experience that changed the way I think about everything. If you'd asked me about angels and miracles before it happened I would have laughed in your face.

It was a Saturday afternoon and a beautiful one at that. The sky was the clearest blue you can imagine. I had decided to take my bicycle and go for a long bike ride in the country. As I pedalled along I felt the breeze against my face. I felt so alive, so happy. I hadn't felt this good for ages. Last year I'd started work on a women's fashion magazine. At first I'd loved the buzz of life in the fast lane but the long hours were starting to get to me, as was the job.

I felt like a hypocrite. I loved the glamour and excitement of my job but from day one a part of me felt uncomfortable and uneasy. All the models commissioned by my editor were painfully thin. I'd suffered from anorexia in my early teens but managed to pull through it with the love and support of my family.

As I cycled I began to get a strange, indescribable feeling. It wasn't illness or fear but an extraordinary, indefinable sensation – nothing I can actually describe. Yet I could feel something.

I kept pedalling at a moderate pace and then relaxed as my bike glided downhill. I felt elated as I sped downhill. I lifted both my feet in the air. Eventually I got to the bottom of the hill and started to pedal again at a moderate pace, wondering where the windy road ahead would take me. After cycling for a few moments I heard a voice – and it sounded like my voice – yelling, 'Stop and change direction.'

I hit the brakes. I looked at the road ahead. It was a typical country road with bumps and lots of twists and turns but nothing I or my bike couldn't handle. But why had I shouted, 'Stop and change direction.' I got off my bike and sat down. Why had I said that? After a few moments reflecting on whether or not I was going mad I got up, gave myself a shake, picked up my bike and cautiously started to ride again.

'Stop!' I heard myself yelling again. 'Change direction.' This time I shouted with such urgency that it made my voice feel slightly hoarse. I got off my bike again. I felt really peculiar now. I was speaking to myself and you know they always say that is the first sign of madness. The elated feeling I had earlier vanished. Perhaps I needed to see a doctor. I figured that the best thing to do was to cut short my bike ride, turn around and head home. I crossed to the other side of the road and, still feeling puzzled and disorientated, began to walk, pushing my bike alongside me. I was nervous about getting back on as it somehow seemed to trigger my strange speaking episodes.

When I got to the bottom of the hill it looked so steep I just couldn't face the prospect of walking back up. I suddenly felt incredibly tired so I got my mobile and asked my boyfriend to come and get me. I gave him the name of the road I was on and he said he'd be there within half an hour.

I pulled my bike off the side of the road and decided to eat some of the snacks I had packed. I was ravenous and they tasted delicious. Once I'd finished I started to think about what I'd said to myself on the bike. Perhaps it was time to change direction in a less literal way? I wasn't happy in my job. It wasn't giving me a sense of purpose or meaning. I thought about how I'd always wanted to become a nurse when I was little and then I thought about how a wonderful dietician had helped me see food as a friend not an enemy. I realized then that what I really wanted to do was to learn all about nutrition. I wanted to be a part of the movement to help people take better care of their bodies with healthy food. I felt so excited that I found myself standing up and punching the air. It was one of those real 'ah ha,' moments.

Then I peered up the hill and saw a dark car driving down at quite a speed. I started to wave as I thought it was my boyfriend. I soon realized that it wasn't so I retreated to the side of the road. The car stopped all the same and I saw a man get out. He told me to get into the car. I said I was fine and I was just stopping for a spot of lunch. He started to walk towards me. I screamed and tried to get away but I hadn't expected this. He put his hand over my mouth. I bit his hand. He slapped me. He was dragging me towards his car. I had never known terror like this before. I kicked and screamed as much as I could but there was no one around to hear me.

Then I heard brakes screech and a voice shouting. My boyfriend was wrestling with the guy. Dazed and bleeding I looked around for something to hit the man with as he was overpowering my boyfriend. I picked up a branch on the road, ran towards them and hit the man as hard as I could. I knocked him out.

My boyfriend got up and took me in his arms. 'Hey, I was the one who was supposed to be rescuing you. That was quite a blow. You're stronger than you think.'

I flexed my arms to show off my biceps. Then the reality of what happened hit us both. We were both bruised with cut lips and there was an unconscious man on the floor. My boyfriend called for the police and went into his car to get some rope to tie him up. Five or so minutes later the police arrived to take statements from us all. They told me that it was a godsend I had decided to turn back and call my boyfriend to pick me up. If I hadn't changed direction what might have happened to me doesn't bear thinking about.

I told the police everything, but I didn't tell them about the voice I had heard and how it had been my voice. I haven't even told my boyfriend and it is such a relief to tell someone now. I truly believe that angels can come in many forms and that day I learned that flashes of intuition can also be miracles. My life changed direction in more ways than one after that bike ride. I'm a fully qualified nutritionist now, working in a busy clinic. Although there are ups and downs, as there are in any career, I feel in my gut that I have found my purpose in life.

Many people report flashes of insight when they are in a potentially life-or-death situation but what makes Glenda's story stand out for me is that her intuition recognized danger a good half an hour or so before it happened. So was this just the survival instinct? Or was an angel using Glenda's voice to speak? Glenda believes an angel saved her life that day and talks to them whenever she goes cycling.

This is another story about a girl whose life was saved by the voice of a guardian angel. Pippa sent in this story and I'll let her tell you what happened herself.

Listen to Me

My father was dying. His cancer had spread quickly from his throat and now to his brain. The operation he'd had a week ago was his last hope but when the surgeons opened up his skull they discovered that the tumour was inoperable. We'd all been told to prepare for the worst. My dad had at most weeks and more likely days to live.

I went to see my father as much as I could during the day when the kids were at school. It was horrible leaving him in the afternoon as I didn't know if he'd be alive when I returned the next morning. He was so thin and weak. He couldn't eat anything. He was dying before my eyes.

Even though he must have been in agony he still made every effort to stay cheerful and upbeat. He told me that he was looking forward to putting his feet up in heaven and finishing that game of chess with my mum. She'd died suddenly from a stroke. They'd been playing chess the night before and my father had left the chess pieces in exactly the same place ever since. He told me that he was just about to checkmate her.

One morning – I remember it clearly because it was the day before my 45th birthday – I composed myself and stepped into his room trying hard to smile. 'Hi dad,' I said, 'Remember me?'

My dad seemed even weaker than usual. His breathing was heavy and laboured. I started to talk to him about Sophie – his precious granddaughter. I didn't know if he heard me but every now and again he smiled weakly.

Tears stung my eyes. That day was tough. Somehow I knew this was the end of the road for dad. I knew he didn't want me to collapse so I tried to be as strong as I could. When it came to school pick-up time I sat on his bed and leaned into his chest for one final cuddle. He raised his hand and patted my back just as he always did when I was little.

I couldn't help myself; I started to sob hysterically. After a few minutes my father raised his head off the pillows and kissed my forehead. He asked me if there was anything I needed to know before he died.

I was shocked. This was the first time he had ever mentioned death. We all knew it was coming but we preferred to avoid it. I started to say that he was talking nonsense and I would see him in the morning but he shook his head slowly from side to side. Then he asked me again if I had any questions.

'Yes,' I replied. 'Find a way to let me know that you haven't gone. I need to know you are okay.'

'Now, that's a challenge,' he said with a hint of a smile on his face. 'Are there any other questions or requests?'

I shook my head and hugged him again, telling him I would see him tomorrow.

I started to gather my things to leave and as I did my dad told me that it was his turn now and he had something he needed to ask me. 'Now listen to me,' he said. 'I don't want Sophie to play over at Monica's house on Friday after school.' It was a strange request. Sophie had been invited round to play at Monica's and have a sleepover and she was very excited, but here was my dad pleading for her to stay at home. I didn't understand the request and I didn't know how my dad even knew about it but I said okay.

Sophie was furious when I told her I had cancelled her play date for no good reason at all. She cried and cried but I had promised my dad. I reassured Sophie and told her that Monica could come and stay with us instead. Sophie took a while to come around to the new plan but eventually relented.

The next day when I went into hospital my dad had slipped into a coma. The doctors said they had no idea how long he would be like this but if it lasted over a week I should consider shutting off his life support. I was devastated but also relieved that dad was no longer in pain. Yet I couldn't bring myself to turn off his life-support machine. I wasn't ready to let him go.

On Friday Monica came round for the sleepover. I had thought of cancelling it but Sophie had been having a rough time recently and I figured some midnight games and snacks would do her the world of good. When Monica's mum Margaret came round to collect her on Saturday morning she was covered in red marks and swellings.

I asked her what had happened and she told me that it was a blessing Monica had been over at mine because at about 4 pm on Friday she had come home as normal and put the television on. While she was in the kitchen making a cup of tea she noticed some bees buzzing around the light bulbs. She tried to shoo them out with a dishcloth but as she did more and more bees appeared. Soon they were everywhere in the kitchen and in the living room. She got her son out as quickly as possible but he was still stung twice on the arm.

The council sent workers around with masks and bee-repellent clothing and they sprayed her house, killing all the bees, which apparently had been nesting for several weeks in her air conditioning unit.

When I heard Maggie's story I gasped. Sophie was allergic to bee stings and the consequences could have been fatal if she had been exposed to a nest of them. Then it dawned on me – my father's odd request to have the girls around at my house instead of Maggie's could well have saved Sophie's life.

That Saturday afternoon after visiting dad in hospital I went round to his flat. The doctors were not pressuring me but I could sense that they wanted me to sign papers to turn off his life support. As I unlocked the door I could smell cigars just as I always used to when I visited dad. He wasn't a big smoker but every night after dinner he would enjoy a cigar or two. I looked around at all the familiar objects and photographs. I went to his cupboard and smelled his clothes. Then I made myself a cup of tea in his favourite mug and sat down. 'Thank you, dad,' I said under my breath. I wasn't just thanking him for keeping Sophie safe from the bees but for being the best dad in the world.

I looked at the chess set on the coffee table. It was still set up in the middle of play as my dad wanted it to be. I knew exactly where each piece lay as I had sat here so many times. Tears came into my eyes and I wiped them away but when I looked back something had changed. The black knight had moved. It was now checkmating the white queen. My dad was here with me. He was giving me the sign he promised and also telling me it was time to let him go. However, instead of feeling sad I felt light and calm.

I left my father's flat and headed straight to the hospital. I held my dad's hand as he slipped away but I knew that he had already slipped away several hours before. I know because he had been there with me in his flat.

In this account the love of a grandfather was able to protect his precious granddaughter from danger. His insight was able to work a miracle and to this day Pippa thanks the angels and her father in spirit for the unexplainable gift of his insight.

I'm often asked if people we know can be angels. In the next chapter – where we'll explore both traditional and non-traditional angel sightings – you'll see that although humans are not actually angels they can sometimes be guided by a higher power to save or transform the lives of others. In much the same way loved ones who have passed away are not angels in the traditional sense, but they can act as our guardians, giving us comfort and support when we need it and on occasion saving our lives.

But it isn't just dangerous circumstances or events that angels can save us from. As the next two stories show, angels can also save us from ourselves. I'll let Elaine explain:

Back on Track

I was a rebellious and angry teenager. My 13-year-old brother had died from a brain tumour and I went off the rails. My parents were numb with grief and I was sent to live with my aunt. I hated her. I started to get into trouble a lot and by the time I was 17 I was into drink, drugs and shoplifting. I wasn't a bad person as such. I was just frightened of becoming an adult when my brother had been denied the chance. My tough and bad-ass attitude gave me a false sense of security.

I'm 25 now and feel that my life has got back on track, but something helped me to grow up fast.

It was a Friday night. I was drinking with some mates and although I was tipsy I wasn't at that point when I didn't know what was going on. Even so, I was still in the mood for thrill-seeking so on my way to my friend's house I jumped down onto the train tracks. I shouted to my friends to come down and join me, telling them we could all walk along the tracks as they ran right behind where we needed to be.

My friends started to scream at me. I laughed and called them all chickens. What I didn't know is that my friends could see a train approaching fast. The next thing I knew, some boy had jumped onto the tracks and was dragging me to the side. At this point everything seemed to go into slow motion as if I was being allowed time to think and to act.

Anyway, I stumbled and my foot went in between two live rails. Not only was a train speeding towards me but I had made things worse and put the life of the boy who was trying to save me in danger. I have no idea what happened next, but the next thing I remember is lying flat on the side of the tracks with the train speeding past. In a state of shock I looked at the boy and he wasn't a stranger at all; he was my brother. I started to cry like a baby but when I looked up my brother wasn't there; my friends were. I didn't stop crying for days. I cried for my brother and I cried for myself and the person I was becoming. From that moment on I grew up a lot.

None of my friends saw the mystery boy who saved my life but I know it was my brother. Whenever I am on a train now I look down at the small space between the live tracks and remind myself how fortunate and blessed I am to be alive.

Like Elaine, Arthur's greatest enemy was himself.

Seeing a Light

My name is Arthur. I never thought I'd admit to this but I was once an alcoholic. In the summer of 2000 I lost my job and my wife of seven years left me. I though I had nothing to live for except the bottle.

On the day my divorce papers came through I went to the off licence and bought as many bottles of wine and gin and cans of beer as I could. On the way home with the bottles and cans clinking a cyclist flew past me and sprayed mud all over me. I lost my balance and fell to the side of the road onto my bags of drink. Several bottles broke and there was glass everywhere. I tried to salvage as much as I could, cutting my fingers in the process, but it was hopeless.

All of a sudden I felt as though something was pouring out of me through my head. The sensation was so great that I held my head in my hands. Then I heard a high-pitched sound in my ear and in the corner of my eye I saw a little light – a small, very bright light that got larger and larger. I wasn't scared, just amazed. The light touched me above my heart. I jumped a little because I was startled. The place where I was touched became a warm spot that seemed to travel throughout my entire body. As the warmth spread, I lost my taste for alcohol.

I am certain that an angel came to me that day. My life has changed. I've rebuilt my life and I've been sober for eight years and counting. I've got a new job and a new partner and life couldn't be better. That experience changed my life. It was a miracle. I have told this story only to my closest friends. Some believe me while some do not, but this is definitely what happened.

I couldn't think of a better way to conclude this chapter than with Ian's remarkable story.

High Flier

I've wanted to tell other people this story many times, but for some reason I've always held back. I guess I'm frightened of their reaction. They might think I'm crazy or something but I can assure you I'm not. I'm a level-headed human resources officer. I like routine, order and logic. I'm more interested in this world than the next.

Anyway, a few months ago I was on my usual February skiing vacation. I was about six when I put on my first pair of skis. I'm 46 now and have only had a break from skiing for one year when work made it impossible to take my vacation at my usual time. I've been very fortunate. I've never had a broken bone or ankle. I guess it's because I'm not reckless. I'm not a cautious skier but I know when to slow down.

Anyway, I was on this really steep slope when I got separated from my friends. I realized that I was barrelling down the hill too fast so I tried to slow down by changing direction. This seemed to make me go even faster. I was zooming towards a clump of trees and I couldn't alter my course. I knew I was going to crash. The trees were getting closer by the second. But then something stopped me. I heard a thud and then everything was quiet.

I hadn't crashed and I hadn't lost consciousness. I was just sitting down on the snow and someone was helping me to stand. I looked up and a boy in a white cap and white jacket was in front of me. He had the clearest blue eyes I have ever seen and they were looking directly into my eyes. They were so radiant that I had to blink – it was as if I was looking directly into the sun. I won't forget what he said. 'Sometimes you've got to speed up to slow down. You're going to be fine. You don't have to worry; just take some time to get your bearings.'

I closed my eyes and started to take some deep breaths. When I opened them the boy was gone. I called out and looked for him but he had vanished. There were no markings in the snow. Had I met my guardian angel or was I hallucinating? I guess I'll never know.

A few weeks later I missed out on a promotion that I had worked for and deserved. I remembered the words of that boy on the mountain and instead of quietly getting on with my job I signed up with a headhunter and found a new job within months. It was quite a risky thing for me to do as I'd been in my job for 25 years since I left school and I had a lot to lose, but I don't regret my decision. I love my new job. Thanks to my angel, I'm living life to the full – in the fast lane.

Perhaps Ian will never know if he was saved by an angel or not. He doesn't know the answer but what he does know is that he found something miraculous by remembering the magnificent soul with gentle, friendly eyes who saved his life.

Having had personal experience of being saved by an angel from certain death it is hard not to wonder why help comes to one person and not another, why here, why me, why now. I've come to the conclusion that this is one unfathomable mystery that humans will never be able to understand. What I do know for sure is that sometimes miraculous things happen to ordinary people when they least expect it and sometimes angels – either in their divine form or in the form of other people – can lift us up and carry us along when the going gets tough. In the process they leave not just the person involved, but everyone who hears their story, in a state of questioning wonder that can change their lives forever.

CHAPTER 6

Angels in this Life and the Next

Every man contemplates an angel in his future self.

Ralph Waldo Emerson

Under the guidance of angels, the spirits of departed loved ones can touch our lives, so in this book I've often referred to spirits as angels, even though angels aren't strictly speaking spirits. Angels are unique. They have never had a physical life here on earth, so they have never known negative emotions. They are simply pure beings of love.

From the very first spark of life we are blessed with a guardian angel and if we follow our intuition – the voice of our guardian angel – we can find fulfilment and happiness. Unfortunately, we often give in to negative emotions and when this happens it is all too easy to stop listening to our intuition. But when we sit calmly and quietly and take time to listen, our guardian angel is always there to help us make decisions, influencing us through dreams and hunches.

Angels can be found in all the major world religions, but they aren't tied down to any one in particular. Whether you are religious or not, they will still watch over you but, because we have free will, they can't intervene if you are not willing to open your mind and believe in the impossible. There isn't a day that goes by when I am not amazed by the sheer number of people who have taken that leap of faith and opened their minds and hearts to their guardian angels. The stories in this chapter are from people who believe they have met angels both in this life and the next. Sometimes these angels take animal or human form but later on you'll read some incredible accounts from people who believe they actually saw angels in their divine form. Some of these accounts will stretch your belief as they have stretched mine but when you read them let your feelings, not your logic, be your judge. Surprise yourself!

Loving Animal Angels

If you've ever loved an animal you'll know what a positive impact they can have on your life. When I was about three years old I was given a black and white cat for my birthday. Her name was Roddy and from the moment I saw her muddy eyes and delicate features a loving bond grew between us. Almost every night she would creep into my bedroom and cuddle up beside me, purring heavily and playing piano on the bedclothes with her paws.

Roddy was hit by a car 16 years later. She survived and tried so hard to hang on but was in such pain that the only option was to have her put down. She died two weeks before I was due to leave home for the first time to study at university. I felt nervous about this new phase in my life. I was excited but a part of me didn't want to grow up and leave home. Roddy's death seemed like a sign from the heavens that it really was time for me to move forward. She'd been my constant companion all these years and now that I was ready to fly it was as if her task on earth was done.

In the first few weeks and months after leaving home I was terribly homesick. I'd often wake up crying in the middle of the night and I'd doze back to sleep convinced that my cat was snuggling up next to me, padding the blankets as she always used to when she was alive. I remember once being absolutely convinced she was in bed with me. I switched on the light and when I looked down there was a football-sized shape dent on the bed where I had felt her cuddling up next to me. (And no, before you ask there wasn't any other person in bed with me at the time!)

I've been contacted by owners of many different types of animals with similar stories of how they continue to sense or feel their presence long after they had gone. Why does this happen? The reason is simple. The spirits of animals we have loved continue to visit because love is the most powerful force in the universe. It cannot be broken by death.

As this story sent to me by Shirley shows, even after our beloved pets have died, they can come back and visit us at any time.

Sasha

It was on a Friday afternoon that our lovely nine-year-old golden retriever Sasha died. She went for a run in the garden and had some kind of heart attack. It all happened so quickly that I didn't have any time to prepare or grieve.

My only consolation was that at least Sasha hadn't suffered much and if you are going to die, what better way than after a lazy, sunny afternoon chasing butterflies in the garden with the flowers in bloom. Even so, I wasn't prepared for the grief I would feel. I'd never owned a pet before Sasha. I got her a year after my divorce and she had definitely filled a void in my life. Instead of spending my evenings drinking and wallowing in self-pity, I had Sasha to walk and train. Instead of walking alone I had Sasha to walk with. She was more than a dog to me. She was a lifesaver.

The day after she passed I could actually feel her presence around me. My friends thought I was going crazy. They urged me to get rid of Sasha's things but I couldn't. When I held her collar I could point to the place in the room where I felt she was sitting.

At night I could feel her jumping onto the end of my bed. Sasha loved sleeping there. Then about a week later I could feel her brushing against my leg. I would go into the garden and see a white ball of light flashing around chasing butterflies. Sasha used to chase butterflies in the garden – always – and she was still chasing them after her passing.

I felt Sasha's presence for about three months. Then one day my boss called round to see me. He brought his white poodle with him. He told me that he needed to work abroad for six months and needed someone to look after Poppy. He told me that he would understand completely if I didn't feel ready, but he wanted to ask me first as he knew I loved dogs. I could tell right away that Poppy was aware of Sasha's presence in the room with us. Poppy growled and barked and looked at the corner of the room where Sasha always used to sleep. The growling went on for about ten minutes. Then all of a sudden Poppy stopped growling, walked over and laid down in the very same spot, curled up and went to sleep perfectly content. I felt I was being given a message from Sasha that she was happy in spirit and that she wanted me to be happy too.

The occurrences stopped a few days later. I think Sasha has gone over to the other side and that getting Poppy to sleep in her spot was her way of reaching me. I have felt better about her death since then, and know that we will be together again someday. I did take care of Poppy for six months and, although she could never replace Sasha, and I don't think I'll own another dog again, I enjoy having dogs in my life so much that I've become a kind of foster mum for dogs when their owners need to vacation or travel for work. Right now I'm looking after two dogs and a third is due to arrive for a six-week stay tomorrow.

John, who is the husband of one of my closest friends, sent me this next account. I adore this story because it clearly shows that as long as there is love the connection between an owner and a pet is unbreakable.

Martin

My wife Rebecca and I shared nine years of our lives with our beloved dog Martin, an Alsatian. He was our first child really and our best friend. He was so full of life and energy and love.

Martin was about a year old when we first brought him home. He was so tiny, frail and underweight that he looked like a newborn. The dogs' home we collected him from told us that he had been abused as a puppy. He had been left outside all day and all night by his owner with three other dogs who were older and more aggressive. They had eaten all his food, so he had chewed on items containing lead-based paint and then started to suffer seizures. The kennel owner suggested that I take a healthier dog home but there had been an instant connection when I looked into Martin's eyes and I knew he was going to come home with me.

In the nine glorious years we had him he suffered uncomplainingly through the treatment for his poisoning. He was as steadfast a companion as life could offer. He never complained as he travelled around the UK with us. We were both lawyers and travelled to where the work was. He enjoyed chasing a ball, though I always felt he was humouring me, because nine times out of ten he would get distracted by birds flying overhead or daisies in the fields.

I always knew that Martin's life expectancy would be shortened by the abuse he suffered as a puppy but it was still a shock when about a year before his death his legs started to crumple underneath him. The vet told me he had neural failure in his back legs which meant he had problems shifting one limb in front of the other. The vet was unwilling to say when the pain would end. My wife and I discussed it and we couldn't bear to be Martin's executioners. We loved him like he was our child.

A few months later Martin's front legs began to crumple too and it was pitiful to watch him trying to drag himself along the ground. It was my wife who finally called the vet – she's always been stronger than me – and the vet agreed to come round the following day.

I slept fitfully with him on the floor of the front room on his last night. I didn't want to cut short any of the remaining time I had with him. When we got up I fretted over his breakfast and then I remembered the futility of it all. He would be dead before it was digested. Half an hour to go and he snored loudly with his head on my lap as I stroked his head. I felt like a traitor. I heard the vet arrive. Martin was panting with pain by now trying to get his body to stand. I rubbed him and started to cry. I felt selfish as I cried, as I should have been the strong one – supporting him. I picked Martin up and took him upstairs into the spare room which over the years had become Martin's room. All his favourite things were there. I opened the window and a refreshing breeze hit my face.

I heard the vet and my wife coming up the stairs. There were just moments left. The vet was a kind and gentle woman and she told me exactly what to expect. Martin didn't struggle when he was given the injection. His soft eyes gazed into mine and then began to glaze over. I held him tight, consoled by the fact that he was with someone who loved him. Yet when I took off his collar I felt as if I had betrayed him.

I carried Martin downstairs. We buried him in our garden. Afterwards the house was so quiet my wife and I decided to drive down to some fields nearby to get some fresh air. We'd often taken Martin there. We were both silent as we got into the car and when we arrived I felt tears spring into my eyes. I turned the engine off and my wife gave me a reassuring hug. We sat there for quite a while. We didn't get out of the car; we both just needed time and space to think about Martin. Even though Rebecca kept telling me I'd done the right thing, and deep down inside I knew she was right, I still couldn't help but feel that I had betrayed him. Eventually we decided to leave. I turned the engine on and the radio started to play. I remember thinking it was strange as the radio hadn't been on when we drove there. What was even more astonishing was that the song playing was 'Cruel to be Kind (in the Right Measure)'. I smiled at the coincidence. It really was as if Martin was sending me a message.

Even more miraculous, Rebecca got pregnant a week after Martin died. We'd been trying for years to have a baby and after three unsuccessful attempts at IVF had decided that becoming parents wasn't our destiny. She had a tough first trimester and our doctor was unsure if the pregnancy would last. I was terribly anxious but Rebecca never was. She said she knew everything would be fine. She told me that she'd had a dream of Martin and that she believed he was our baby's guardian angel and always would be. David Martin was born the following March and is now a healthy and happy two-and-a-half years old.

Sometimes I'm convinced that little David is playing with Martin. He'll often head straight for his grave, even though there is no gravestone on it, and play near it watching the daisies and trying unsuccessfully to catch butterflies just like Martin used to.

Stories from ordinary people, like John and Rebecca, whose pet has come back to reassure or visit them from the other side, are heart-warming proof, if proof were needed, that love in whatever shape or form transcends death.

Our pets can teach us much about the power of love, not just in the next life but in this one. In life they are often able to hear and sense and see things that we can't. Many people believe that they have a highly developed intuition or sixth sense and are able to tell when we are in danger. Once again there doesn't seem to be any lack of stories about this phenomenon. Here's a fantastic example sent to me a few years ago by Matilda.

Frosty the Life-Saving Cat

I knew becoming a mum of triplets would be tough but I had no idea. My three daughters weighed just five pounds each and the only clothes I could get to fit them were baby doll clothes. I had my work cut out for me.

Thankfully, when I brought them home from hospital I had a lot of help from my family. Both my mother and my mother-in-law were on a rotation shift of three days and my sister and brother were on standby too. Everyone pitched in and for the first six months the house revolved around the triplets. They ate every two to three hours and the whole day seemed to be taken up with feeding and changing and cleaning. Most nights the only time we had free was a three-to-four-hour break from 7 pm after we put them in their cots. There was never enough time in the day to do everything or think about anything. We needed a full-time cook, cleaner, nanny and organizer. What we had was Frosty, the family cat.

We had never intended to own a cat but when we found this little kitten in a cardboard box one day dumped in our street we didn't have the heart to take her to the kennels. We knew that it was highly unlikely anyone would want her. She wasn't ugly but her marking wasn't appealing. It was like somebody had dropped a pot of white paint on her; she was a mess. But we grew to love having that mess around. I was perhaps the fondest of her and during my pregnancy her comforting purring helped me through many a sleepless night.

Frosty was besotted with the triplets as soon as we brought them home. We'd read up about cats and babies and the risk of suffocation and disease so we did all we could to keep them apart. I could tell that the rejection upset Frosty but she soon learned that the triplets were a no-go area.

When the triplets were about four months old and we were finally starting to settle into a routine of sorts Frosty broke the rules we had set and in the process saved our lives. I'd noticed in the weeks previously that a lot of the flowers we had been sent were dying fairly quickly but my brain was far too lethargic to make any connections. I'd been suffering from headaches and back pain for the past few weeks and they were really slowing me down.

It was about 2 pm and I was using some of my sacred free time to email friends with updates on my progress. Suddenly, Frosty leapt up on my desk as she often does, but her behaviour wasn't normal. She kept licking her paws roughly as if something was biting them. I took her on my lap and checked her paws to see if she had been bitten or scratched but there wasn't any dirt or sign of infection there. I put her down on the floor and she stared to pant loudly, a quick, desperate type of pant with her tongue jutting forward between tiny teeth. It wasn't a constant panting, just short bouts, spasmodic. Then she leapt onto my keyboard and started to dive desperately around on it. I wondered if she was on heat and picked her up to take her to the cat flap so she could roam outside. As soon as I got there she eagerly jumped outside.

I went back to my desk and my emails but a few minutes later I heard a noise coming from the nursery monitor – it was like a dull thud. I dropped everything and ran upstairs into the triplets' room with my husband and mother-in-law following close behind. When I got to the nursery I saw that the door was wide open and Frosty was inside. To this day I don't know how the door opened. Frosty was on the bookcase knocking books onto the floor. I reached out to grab her but as I did she leapt right into one of the triplet's cots. My heart filled with terror. Frosty was almost sitting on the baby and rolling him around in the crib. I leapt towards the cot to save my baby from what I thought was injury or even worse, when Frosty jumped out and lay down on the floor and started panting again.

After checking that all the triplets were fine I knelt down to pick up Frosty. Holding her in my arms, she was clearly agitated and seemed to be possibly hallucinating as she kept pawing at the air as if a bug was buzzing about before her. Not knowing what was bothering my cat, I rushed Frosty to the vet.

Mercifully, we got an appointment that evening. As soon as the vet had examined Frosty and given her an anti-inflammatory shot which calmed her fairly quickly, he went directly to questions regarding poisoning: could she have gotten into any medications? Had any cleaning supplies been recently used or left out? Could she have lapped at anti-freeze in a nearby gutter?

What puzzled the vet was that Frosty's eyes exhibited normal pupilary response; most household poisons and drugs cause animal pupils to either dilate or contract, or to at least grow sluggish in their response to light. The only other possibility was carbon monoxide poisoning.

In fires, it's rarely the flames that claim lives. Nearly always the actual cause of death is smoke inhalation, specifically carbon monoxide poisoning. Carbon monoxide deprives the body and brain of oxygen, causing the brain to swell and press against the interior of the cranium. The smaller the human or animal, the less brain tissue there is to inflame and the smaller the space available to accommodate the swelling. Thus, the smaller the human or animal, the sooner it will die from the effects. Babies, being so tiny, are especially at risk.

The vet urged me to call home immediately and to get someone to install a carbon monoxide monitor. I told him we had one already and he asked me when we had last changed the batteries. I didn't have any idea and called home to get my mother-in-law to have a check. She phoned back five or so minutes later to tell me that the batteries were flat. She had replaced them and realized immediately that she had to get everyone out of the house. I could hear the siren wailing in the background.

Later, when I called the gas man round I found that there was a fault in our furnace and it was starting to pump not warm, safe oxygen but small amounts of lethal, odourless, colourless carbon monoxide through the floor vents in every room of our home. Had the weather turned cold, I would have turned the furnace on and unknowingly poisoned my entire family. If Frosty had not forced me to take her to the vet after entering the triplets' bedroom I might not be alive today.

Looking back I can see that a lot of Frosty's antics that afternoon were deliberately designed to force me to take action. We were not in any immediate danger that particular day but as soon as the weather turned cold and we started to crank up the furnace we would have been. Her recovery time was too quick and even her desperate panting was an urgent game of charades. Each time she did it was for so short a duration that the purpose was obviously not to cool her down or bring in fresh air. Frosty was pretending to be unwell to get my attention. Frosty was trying to warn me.

Frosty the hero cat now holds a special place in our family. There are no boundaries separating her from the triplets any more as we know that she would never do anything to hurt them – she is their guardian angel. She saved their lives and our lives too. She's a mother of six kittens herself now and everyone is pitching in to assist her. From personal experience I know that when it comes to raising a houseful of kids you need all the help you can get.

Every species of animal, from dogs and cats to rabbits and horses, has much to teach us about love and compassion. Every story I have read attests to the extraordinary courage, devotion and intuition they possess and how their unconditional compassion and love can change lives in unexpected ways. Or, in the case of the remarkable elephant's tale below – sent in by an anonymous hotel worker from Bangkok – they can save lives.

All Creatures Great and Small

There's a resort in Phuket where one of the most sought-after attractions is the elephant ride. There are about ten elephants and each elephant can take up to eight people on its back, first onto the beach, then into the forest and then back to the hotel. It's one of the greatest rides of your life. The elephants are well cared for by the hotel and want for nothing. They are chained to posts when they aren't doing rides. This isn't because they need to be but because it makes them feel safer and protects their children from being trampled during feeding.

About an hour before the first wave hit Phuket during the Boxing-Day tsunami in 2004 the elephants started to get uncharacteristically restless and destructive. About four had just returned from a trip and they hadn't been chained yet by their handler. The four that hadn't been chained helped the others break free from their chains. The handler was powerless to do anything to stop them and by the time he returned with reinforcements they had all climbed a hill and were bellowing. An army of people followed them up the hill to try and get them to return. Then the first wave hit.

When the waves had finally subsided the elephants charged down the hill and started to pick up children with their trunks and run back up the hill. When they had saved all the children they returned for the adults. I've been told that they rescued over 40 people that day. Then they returned to the beach and carried the bodies of four dead children to the top. Not until the task was done did they allow their handlers to come anywhere near them and mount them again.

It's not just domestic pets or wild animals used to human contact that are touched by angels. There are also many stories of angels and spirits using wild animals to communicate messages after a loved one has passed away. Paul's moving story is a touching example.

Crazy Chickens

Seven and a half years ago my wife and I purchased a small farmhouse with a few acres of land in Sussex. We were both tired of the city and wanted a complete life change. Before we moved in the old owners asked if we wanted to keep the six chickens that were housed in the small henhouse alongside the barn. The told us that they laid an egg a day and would more than earn their keep.

My wife was an animal lover and really wanted to keep them but I've always had a fear of birds and especially chickens ever since I was young. I don't know why but they just terrify me. My wife was understanding and decided not to press me on the issue, but every so often she would ask me if I was ready to change my mind. I told her that she was the only crazy chicken I needed and she laughed knowingly.

My wife died unexpectedly on 1 November 2005. There was no warning, nothing. One day she was her usually sunny self and the next she was lying in a hospital bed. They put 'brain tumour' on her death certificate. She was buried in the local church. We had never discussed funeral arrangements but I knew that she would have wanted to be close to her beloved farmhouse. As for me I couldn't face going back to live in the farmhouse without her so I decided to sell up and move closer to the city to be near my family.

My world seemed incredibly empty and meaningless after my wife died. I lost my appetite for life. It was as if I was going through the motions. During the week I'd head to work as usual and in the evenings I'd watch television alone in my flat. At the weekends I'd head back down to the country to visit her grave. It was comforting and painful to be close to her.

One weekend I decided to stop by the old farmhouse to check that it was being well cared for by its new owners; a charming couple called Jane and Derek. I knew this is something my wife would have wanted me to do. Jane and Derek were incredibly welcoming when I knocked on the door and were happy for me to wander around the grounds to gather my memories.

When I went into the backyard the first thing I noticed was that the henhouse door was open. I took a look inside and saw six hens. As soon as they saw me they started to waddle towards me. Surprisingly, I wasn't afraid. The six hens were very tame and one of them – the largest – came right up to me. I smiled, thinking of my wife and how she would have loved this moment. Then I turned around and the large hen followed me. It followed me as I wandered around the backyard and each time I stopped it stopped too, with its head bolting from side to side.

Realizing I couldn't shake off the hen I picked her up and put her back in the henhouse, closing the door behind me. Half an hour or so later when I was ready to leave I went back to thank Jane and Derek for allowing me to visit. I felt happier than I had done for months. When I told them about the chicken incident they couldn't believe their ears. First of all they corrected me by saying that the hen that followed me wasn't a hen at all – it was a cock they had called Crazy Red because he would never let anyone go near him. They told me I must have a real affinity with animals. Derek even showed me some scratches on his hands and arms when he had tried to pick Crazy Red up. He showed me the thick gloves he had to wear every time he needed to handle him.

I knew then with a certainty that I can't explain fully that my wife was making contact with me. She wanted me to ditch my fear not just of birds, but of loving and living again.

Stories about animal angels could fill a book by themselves but hopefully this brief selection of stories has given you a snapshot of the strong connections that clearly exist between animals and humans. They communicate their love, compassion and wisdom in ways that we don't expect. They don't demand much from us. Like angels, they simply love us and watch over us in this life and the next.

Children Who See Angels

If you ever need a shot in the arm to believe in angels – ask children. Children have the eyesight, the innocence and the trust to see the miraculous that unfortunately many of us gradually lose as we get older. Children still possess the capacity for wonder and open-mindedness.

This is not the same as being gullible or naïve but it does mean not shutting out whatever does not conform to reason and science.

I love hearing children talk about angels. I love how easily they accept and don't question what they see. They tell their angel stories in such a factual way, without a shred of doubt, and if I dare press them for details or clarification they often give me a look a surprise or pity that I need to even ask them to make things clearer. To children it's simple and obvious; guardian angels are real. To parents and carers, however, like Cindy whose daughter Megan can see angels, it can be confusing. Cindy's account mirrors many other accounts I've been sent over the years by mystified parents.

The Lady in the Curtains

One night I was getting my daughter Megan ready for bed – she was about three at the time (she's now nearly five). She waved and smiled across the room at the windows (the curtains were drawn). I asked her what she was looking at and she just pointed to the curtains. I then asked her who she was waving to, and she said, 'The lady.'

We were the only ones in the room at the time, and when I asked her again who she was waving at, she said, 'The lady in the curtain.'

The curtains in Megan's bedroom are pink with purple stripes so with the best will in the world I couldn't see or imagine the shape of a lady there. Megan told me the lady was her angel. She showed no fear whatsoever, and was completely at ease with 'the lady'.

About a year before I had begun to hear Megan talking to someone and when I asked her who she was talking to she would say, 'My angel friends.' I thought she must have what folks call imaginary friends, but I know that they are real to my daughter. I asked her what her friends looked like and she said fairytale princes and princesses. Then, about four or five months back, I walked into the living room and she started laughing as if she had heard the funniest joke and she said, 'You are so funny.'

I didn't know what to think! Another time when we were driving home from the supermarket Megan was looking out the window and talking. She turned to me and said, 'They don't have mums and dads.' She said she wanted to throw her toys in the sky so they could play with them. I asked her again what her friends looked like and she said fairies.

As far as I'm aware, fairies and angels have wings. But whenever she talks to them she's laughing.

The other night I put her to bed and I was outside the bedroom door putting towels away and I heard her say, 'Night, night Nana.' My mother died back in 1992 before Megan was born and my husband's mother died when he was a child. Everyone else tells me that imaginary friends are a phase some children go through but I'm beginning to think she really can see angels. The strange thing is I'm not religious and I've never talked to her about angels.

I've heard countless stories about children who can see angels. Sure, you could dismiss it all as imagination or fantasy but the wonderful thing about children is their ability to suspend disbelief. It is this ability which makes children far more receptive to psychic experiences and angelic visitations than adults.

It is a child's ability to accept unquestioningly that can help a parent determine if their child is having a true angelic experience or simply making things up. In my experience, if a child has seen an angel they will typically feel safe and unafraid. The experience will not unsettle them. Some highly sensitive children may panic the first time they see them, especially if they haven't been introduced to the idea, but after that first meeting there will be no alarm or fear. In fact, your child will feel comforted by their presence, like a warm hug. If, however, they are frightened or unsettled by their experience, it is fear- and not angel-based; it might be time to monitor their exposure to frightening DVDs and TV programmes.

Many children are comforted by being told that their guardian angel is watching over them. Nothing calms my children more at night than when I tell them that their guardian angels are watching over them, catching their bad dreams. Just as it was when I was a child it's become a part of my children's bedtime routine to talk to the angels every night and thank them for their loving guidance.

Although children can see angels whether or not other family members believe in them too, it really helps children talk about their experiences if their parents are open and receptive. Unfortunately, adults can often react to children's stories about angels with fear and distrust and this disturbs and puzzles children very much. Peter's story illustrates this.

Table Dance

I was about nine years old at the time. My mum was in the kitchen cooking dinner and my six-year-old brother came in and said there was a woman dancing on the kitchen table. My mother asked him what he was talking about. When he told her that the woman wanted to speak to her she picked him up, put him on the table and shouted at him that there was no one there. My brother told my mum that the woman said nobody should be afraid of her. This made my mum even angrier. She sent my brother to his room and told him he wouldn't be having any tea that night. She said she had had enough of his story telling.

Later I tiptoed into my brother's room to comfort him. He was lying in bed. He'd been crying and I held him tight. He told me that he wasn't crying because he'd been told off, he was crying because he didn't understand why he had been told off. All the woman had wanted was to let our mum know she was so happy to be her guardian angel that she was dancing on the table to celebrate.

Childhood should be a comforting and magical time but there is no escaping the fact that for some children it can be deeply traumatic, disturbing and dark. Malcolm had this angelic experience when he was a young and vulnerable boy neglected and abandoned by his mother and abused by his stepfather.

Drifting Away

When I was an infant, I was told that my mother would put me in my crib, three floors up, and go downstairs to shoot up … to escape from the pressure. My sister reported that when she got home from school, my nappies would be so badly soiled that I had horrible rashes all the time. She would change me and go downstairs to start dinner. My mother did not want to feed me. So I was fed when my father was home. Since he was working long and hard to make ends meet with two children, eating was a sporadic affair.

My father died when I was two. After that my mother brought home a number of men, each more unsavoury than the last. I did not play and know the joys of childhood the way a normal child would. I wasn't loved and nurtured. I was told all of the time how unlovable I was, and I was told to shut up.

Things were to get far worse, though, when my mother remarried. As soon as rings were exchanged my stepfather took over our house. He had a foul temper. I soon learned to disappear into my room when he was in the house. One night when I was five I heard my mother and stepfather screaming at each other downstairs. I ran into the kitchen and saw her huddled on the floor with blood running down her face. I just stood there saying nothing. He came over to me and told me to keep my mouth shut or else. I was scared, but I didn't think he would actually hurt me. I was only a child.

Over the next year or so I managed to avoid the fists which flew at my mother by retreating into my own head, laying low, and hiding, no, erasing all emotion. I figured I was out of danger since I was a child – I mean, no evil bastard would beat up a child! I had quickly trained myself not to react when I saw him beating my mother into submission. Any reaction from her urged him on so I remained silent and non-responsive.

I remember the feeling I experienced every time I saw him put his fist to my mother's face and watched the blood pour out of her nose and lips. How would she live with such fear and unhappiness and why did she keep running back to him? I knew the meaninglessness of life – I wanted to die in the act of torturing and killing him. I split in two and lost myself entirely.

It was on my seventh birthday that he first turned his anger on me. I was late for school and accidentally bumped into him as I rushed out of the front door. The next thing I remember was staring up at an enormous booted leg which led from my neck to his head and the ceiling beyond. I heard him say, 'You will NOT bump into me. They will carry you out in a body bag.'

He hit me so hard that that I lost consciousness. When I woke up I saw myself lying on the floor and my stepfather kicking me over and over again. I watched it happen. Then I felt warm arms holding me, rocking me. I felt myself drifting away. The next thing I remember is being in hospital.

I never saw my mother or stepfather again after my stay in hospital. I went to a care home for a year and then was put up for fostering. I was told later that when my stepfather had finally gone out I'd managed to crawl to the phone and dial 100 for the police. When they arrived I had crawled to the door and answered it covered in welts and bruises. I have no memory of doing any of this. All I can remember is somehow separating from my body and drifting away in the arms of an angel.

Malcolm is now a happily married father of five. The scars of his past still return to haunt him and he can never forget the pain and fear, but the terrible abuse he suffered has led him to a strong belief in the power of love and angels. He has met up with other victims of child abuse who had similar experiences and he hopes that sharing his story with others who have suffered will be of some comfort. As an adult he doesn't see angels any more but he says he can still feel and sense them all around him. He sees them every day in the faces of his children.

Is it childish and unrealistic to believe in angels? I don't believe it is because the more young at heart we are the more we can let go of our fear, mistrust and doubt so we can hear what the angels are saying. For that is what our angels want – our attention.

Today, news of violence, hatred and injustice has become part of the normal fabric of life, part of our thinking. Our children are getting a terrible and soul-destroying message. Children everywhere need to learn more about the angels, and about love. The world can't give them the answers they need to the questions that upset them, but the angels can give them the sense of certainty and comfort they crave.

Therefore, every parent that encourages their child to ask the angels for guidance is strengthening the power of their child to believe in the power of their own creativity.

Mysterious Strangers

There are many stories about mysterious strangers who appear at just the right moment to help someone in trouble and then vanish without a trace, often without waiting for a thank you. In fact, we have already seen some of these stories in this book. These people are often described as angels, not necessarily because they have angelic faces or appearance but because they perform selfless acts on behalf of others.

Of course, it would be easy to explain all these stories as inspiring examples of human kindness and sacrifice, and in many instances this is exactly the case. However, there are some mysterious stranger stories that are not so easy to explain. In these stories the stranger typically appears from nowhere and disappears afterwards in the same unseen manner. There is often something other-worldly about their appearance, and their ability to have exactly the right resources or solution to a difficult situation is uncanny. They often know things that no one else could know. All this suggests that these mysterious strangers are either angels at work or humans, consciously or unconsciously guided by a higher power.

Could there be any other explanation for Adele's remarkable adventure?

Brief Encounter

I'd been working late and just managed to catch one of the last trains home. I wondered if I was the only passenger on the train. My carriage was completely empty. My stomach started to howl. I'd been so busy at work that I hadn't had time to eat anything all day.

As the train bounced along I glanced up at the destination notice and realized with a shudder that I was on the wrong train. Instead of heading home to Chichester I was going in completely the wrong direction. Worse still, the train wasn't stopping at many stations. There was nothing I could do but sit it out. If I'd had a mobile I would have called home but this was close to 30 years ago.

If this wasn't bad enough things were about to get a whole lot worse. The door between my carriage and the next opened and two men wearing soiled clothes and talking loudly walked through. Weaving and leering down the centre passage they were obviously drunk. They stumbled down the aisle and slumped in the seat opposite mine. They stared at me strangely. They were going to either mug or rape me. Given that I'm only five feet tall I would be no match for them. This is it, I thought, and it's going to be bad. I prayed.

A tall, slender, white-haired gentleman suddenly appeared from the seat behind me. He calmly walked in front of the thugs and sat beside me as if they didn't exist.

He nonchalantly asked me if I was lost and I told him that I was on the wrong train. The man smiled reassuringly and told me not to worry about it and he would make sure I got home safely. He hadn't asked me where I needed to go. He hadn't asked any other questions. Despite the drunken louts in front of me, I suddenly felt safe, even comforted.

The train went on. The intoxicated men looked totally lost and dumbfounded. One of them held his head in his hands as if he had a headache and the other held his stomach as if he was winded. None of them looked at me or him, only at the ground in confusion.

Eventually, the train stopped and the stranger said that I needed to get off here and change trains. I followed him and he took me to one of the station guards. He told them that I needed to get back to Chichester that evening. The guard told me that I was in luck. His wife was picking him up in a few minutes and the two of them were heading down to Chichester to visit relatives. I could travel with them. I thanked the guard and the silver-haired man. He smiled and walked straight down the station platform. I did not see him vanish or anything but everything about his appearance and the effect he had on the thugs and the guard told me that I was being looked after in some way. I've told a lot of people this story and most of them believe that this guy was an angel sent to protect me from certain violence that evening.

Adele could well be right. There are many things about this silver-haired stranger that suggest that he was more than a passing Good Samaritan. First of all, there is the effect he had on the thugs. They were bullies and surely the two of them could have overpowered a young girl and an elderly gentleman? Their confusion and weakness in his presence is a sure sign of his powers. And if that were not enough, how on earth did he know that Adele was lost and where she needed to be going that night? Finally, why hadn't Adele noticed him in the carriage when she came in and walked past rows of empty seats? All in all, there seems nothing ordinary about this mysterious stranger.

There's also nothing ordinary about the mystery man who saved Glen when he was on holiday in South America.

Coming Up for Air

I was on the second week of a fantastic vacation in South America with my girlfriend. We decided to spend the day swimming and sunbathing at a deserted beach. It was a stunning day with a slight breeze and clear blue sky. But there was a powerful undercurrent that made swimming difficult.

As my girlfriend headed out into the sea I found myself fighting to stay on my feet, and I decided to stay in the shallow water that just hit around my ankles. My girlfriend shouted at me to come out further and I told her to give me a few minutes. I'm not a great swimmer as I have a heart condition and – although I would never have admitted it to her – I never felt happy getting my head underwater.

My girlfriend showed off her swimming prowess and kept calling to me to come out with her. Finally, she convinced me to take the plunge and I started to edge closer. I stopped when the water came to my shoulders and splashed around my neck. My girlfriend could see that I was making an effort and joined me, splashing and swimming around.

After a while she decided to head back to the beach to soak up some sunshine. She asked me to come back with her but I told her I would wait for the next wave to push me to shore. To be honest I was tired and finding it hard to stand, let alone swim, and the boost that a wave gave me would see me to dry land safely. My girlfriend nodded, assumed a diving position and swam back to shore. I waited for the wave but instead of being carried to shore, for some reason I was pulled beneath the water and dragged further out to sea.

When I came up for air I was way out of my depth. I couldn't feel the sand beneath my toes. Another wave came and dragged me still further out. Frantically, I tried to swim against the current but my efforts just pushed me further away from shore.

I was terrified that I was going to drown. I gasped for air only to be pulled under by yet another wave. By now the waves were coming so quickly it was a struggle just to keep my head above the water. Then a towering wave pulled me under the surface. I was convinced now that I would be buried under the sea. I didn't want to die. Instantly, I was shot into the air, but it was long enough for me to take a quick breath. I screamed for help. I looked towards the shore. My girlfriend was running towards me. I was pulled under again and it was several seconds before I came back to the surface to breathe. This time I saw a man wading into the water to the left of my girl-friend and shouting at me in Spanish. I think he was wear-ing blue swimming trunks.

I could feel my body getting weaker. I couldn't under-stand Spanish. I went under the water again as another wave hit. Frantically, I tried to swim to shore but once again I was pulled back. The man in blue trunks was still shouting at me in Spanish but this time I understood what he was saying. He told me to swim towards him, not towards the shore. He told me that when the waves hit me I should not fight them but let them take me. I didn't hesitate to follow the man's advice. He had an air of authority and besides, all my efforts to get back to shore had failed. I moved to my left and when the wave hit I stopped fighting it. I came up for air and I could see the man giving me the thumbs-up sign.

After a few moments I realized that I was making slow progress. I was getting closer to the shore. Then I found myself in waist-deep water. I could feel the sand scrunching between my toes. Gasping for breath I looked towards the spot where the man in blue had been standing but he was nowhere.

My girlfriend rushed over to me and helped me onto the beach. She gave me a towel and apologized over and over again for putting me in danger. She thanked God that I was alive and I said a silent prayer of thanks too as I coughed up water.

I asked my girlfriend if she knew where the Spanish man in blue was. I could tell by her perplexed look that she didn't have a clue who I was talking about. She told me that she hadn't seen or heard anyone. We both looked around the beach and it was as deserted as when we arrived; there weren't even footprints in the place where my angel in blue had been standing.

There is of course the possibility that the man in blue who saved Glen was another swimmer on the beach, who just happened to have an expert knowledge of the currents, but all things considered this incident has all the hallmarks of a classic guardian angel story: the helpful, knowledgeable and comforting stranger who appears and vanishes mysteriously.

Whether human or divine, the ever-growing numbers of stories I've heard or read have convinced me that mysterious strangers performing selfless good deeds are most certainly out there. Who knows, one of these strangers might be you! Ordinary people can become guardian angels to other people by performing acts of selfless kindness, compassion and courage. So why not become an angel yourself by letting the angel inside you speak to all other people?

I Saw an Angel

One thing that has become abundantly clear to me in my work is that you do not need to be clairvoyant or 'psychic' to make contact with your guardian angel. Many people don't actually see their angel but are aware of an angelic presence in other ways. For instance:

- The atmosphere of the room may change. You may feel surrounded by a warm glow. The air may seem to be tingling around you with love and calm, or you may feel a rush of energy down your spine.
- A beautiful aroma may suddenly fill the room.
- You may experience feelings of love or an overwhelming sense of deep peace or protection.
- Coloured lights may appear from nowhere. Shafts of brilliant light, or even spheres of colour, may dance in front of you, especially when you are working with the healing angels.

- You may feel the presence of wings brushing against you or enfolding you, or even angelic hands on your shoulders.

- You may become aware of an increase in the number of coincidences that occur in your life. Or your problems may seem to solve themselves – sometimes in the most unexpected ways.

- A mysterious stranger may appear in your life at just the right moment and this stranger may inspire you, comfort you or rescue you from a dangerous situation.

- Perhaps someone you already know becomes a comforter and lifesaver. Other people can become guardian angels by performing acts of bravery and courage to help others in need.

- Angels may appear in reassuring dreams that speak to your heart. Dreams can convey messages from a higher realm.

- In times of need a comforting and reassuring voice from within may speak to you and fill you with optimism and compassion. This voice can help you connect with the love inside you by giving you a sense of purpose and completeness.

Clearly, angels can appear in our lives in many different ways and the list above is by no means complete because no angelic encounter is entirely the same for each person. There are, however, astonishing accounts from people who have actually seen angels in their divine form and these accounts tend to have more similarities. These spectacular accounts are often so extraordinary that it is easy to see why sceptics dismiss them, even though none of the people have any reason to make them up. And in some cases, prior to their angelic visitation they would have described themselves as non-believers or sceptics.

I suppose it is human nature to question and to doubt. Whenever I recite stories of angelic visitations I can virtually guarantee that the first response I'll get is sceptical. 'Is this real?' 'Is this all right?' My reply is always the same. Any experience that uplifts, helps, heals, inspires, enlightens and adds richness, colour and goodness into a person's life is angelic. And any story that encourages us to open our minds and shows us that the world is a magical place, filled with astonishing things, is a divine blessing.

Take Sherron's story, for example. Some might argue that there is a technical explanation for what she saw or that something 'misfired' in her brain, but Sherron is in no doubt that her life-changing vision was spiritual. And I have no reason to doubt her.

Angels in the Sky

It wasn't winter or nighttime when I witnessed something so extraordinary that it changed my life. I wasn't depressed or on drugs or medication and prior to my vision I hadn't really had any interest in the spiritual side of life. I used to go to church every Sunday when I was a child but as soon as I left home and got my own job and flat I stopped going. The reason I never paid much attention to the spiritual was that I was far more interested in what goes on in the human mind. I'm a psychologist, you see.

I guess any account that you read of a personal experience is only as valid or as honest as the person relating it. What can I tell you about myself? I'm a full-time psychology lecturer and mother of three but I also have a secret life as a Samaritan. In other words I do a lot of phone work and have gone through the gruelling selection process to man the phones. I've never taken drugs and I don't drink. I'm frequently called up in court to give my testimony and am regarded as a reliable witness. All of this is true but I guess those who read my story will either believe me or think I'm making this all up.

At the end of the day my psychology training has taught me that most of what we glean from others is filtered through our own personal experience. So I will just tell you what happened to me and leave you to make your own mind up.

As I said it was a bright summer morning that I took my dog Millie for a walk in the park. My head was filled with my latest case. I was working with a man who suffered the most dangerous and self-destructive depression. I'd tried everything with him but felt now that the only option was to advise that he should be sectioned before he harmed himself. This guy wasn't my only patient but his presence loomed large in my mind as I didn't think he would pull through.

Millie ran for a stick I had thrown and as I watched her rush into the distance I heard the murmur of muted voices in the distance. I looked around and saw nothing, but the voices were coming nearer. It was then that I realized the sounds were not only behind me but above and all around me.

How can I describe the way I felt? It's not easy but it was like a surge of joy that lifted me up. It's really hard to record this floating feeling without sounding like you've taken something. Slightly to my left and about six feet away from me I saw a group of glorious-looking people. They glowed and shone with spiritual loveliness. I just stood there and stared. There were three of them; two were beautiful women dressed in flowing white dresses and their long brown hair floated down their backs. The man was also dressed in white and his hair was white. The group looked like they were engaged in conversation. They didn't seem to be aware of me at all. I could see all their faces very clearly and one woman in particular was so beautiful it made tears fall down my cheek. She was talking intently to the younger woman.

I could hear their singing voices clearly but I could not understand a word they were saying. It was like trying to hear people talking from behind a glass screen. They floated above me in a circle going around and around. There was constant movement. I had a good look at all of them. Their eyes were blue one moment and green the next. They floated away from me and their voices grew fainter until they faded away completely and all I could see was the clear blue sky they had danced in. I stood for several minutes with my feet rooted to the spot. I could see that Millie had done the same. She was sitting down about 15 feet away from me staring intently at the sky. I was glad she had seen it too.

I pinched myself to check I wasn't dreaming until my skin felt red and painful. What I had seen was real. I wasn't mad and I wasn't imagining things. I had seen angels.

I've reported this story as accurately and as truthfully as I would make a statement on a witness stand. But even as I write these words down I can see how extraordinary it sounds. Perhaps the only thing I can say about it is that it changed my life completely. Before my vision I saw the world in black and white. I dealt with the here and now; the material and what is. I can now see that humans have a deep and powerful need for spiritual connection and if you take that away from them their lives lack purpose, fulfilment and colour. The guy I was treating at the time made a full recovery within a month of my vision. I didn't raise an eyebrow when he told me he was listening to the voice of his guardian angel and he didn't feel so empty any more. I believed him. Perhaps that's all he really needed; someone to listen to and believe in him.

Like Sherron, Duke is also convinced that he didn't imagine seeing an angel when he was a child.

Statue of Liberty

I was five years old when I saw my angel. I remember everything from that day crystal clear and I also know within my heart that I did not imagine it. My father died in July of that year and on 2 September it was his birthday. We went down to the cemetery to lay some flowers and say a prayer. When we arrived at my dad's grave my mum bent down to arrange the flowers. I could see that she was crying but trying to hide her tears from me. I wanted to cuddle her but something made me look straight up into the sky. I saw an angel that was the size (or seemed to be) of The Statue of Liberty. It seemed to glow like a pearl light bulb, only more bright and beautiful. It was dressed in a long gown, covering its feet, and had fantastically large wings tucked in behind its back and a book in its hands from which the same golden glowing light was being emitted.

I couldn't tell you if the angel was a man or a woman. The light was so bright it blinded me and I couldn't see things very clearly. When I covered my eyes to shield them from the light the vision vanished.

Over the years I've often pondered the meaning of this visit from the heavens and not really made sense of it until recently. Last year on the 20th anniversary of my dad's death my mum told me that even though she hadn't said so at the time, my vision had given her the most extraordinary comfort and reassurance.

Duke's account has striking similarities to Wendy's. She emailed this surprising story to me a few months ago.

Shooting Star

I was especially close to my aunt when I was growing up. My mother died when I was born and my father raised me as best he could, but on many occasions I lived with my aunt. She didn't have any children of her own and she became the mother I had never known. She was perhaps the most important person in my life when I was growing up. She died when I was 18. She died the most unnecessary death. She had choked on a fish bone. I wasn't prepared for the sorrow that flowed through me. I was overwhelmed with grief.

In the first few months when nothing would stop my tears I would often visit my aunt's grave. My aunt had only been 62 when she died and I was angry with God for taking her away from me when I still needed her. Every day I would sit by her grave and ask God why he couldn't give me my aunt back. One day when I arrived it was starting to rain slightly. My eyes stung from my tears. I looked up at the cloudy sky and once again expressed my anger to the heavens.

At that moment I saw what looked like a shooting star coming out of the clouds. It wasn't bright or white. It looked grey like the clouds it came from. The shooting star danced in and out and around the clouds. I was convinced my eyes were playing tricks on me. Then the star headed towards me and out of it an image appeared. I nearly fell over backwards; all the breath left my body. The angel that appeared had grey wings and a grey robe. There was a heavy cord tied around her waist; at least I think it was a she. I'm not sure. What dazzled me most though was the bright light surrounding her. I couldn't see her face as her wings stretched all around her. She had her hands reaching upwards with her palms facing towards heaven. I fell to my knees.

The angel was real, of that I am sure. There was no face and I couldn't tell if it was male or female but it was the most brilliant and powerful thing. I can't tell you how but it made me feel as if it had power over my life. The wings looked so strong and I'm guessing if I stood by the angel it would be about nine feet tall. I was afraid but in awe at the same time. I knew I was seeing an angel. The light surrounding it was so bright, so intense. The angel's hands reached towards me and I could tell that my presence was being acknowledged. Then the angel's wings spread wide around its body before snapping back to its sides, making a crashing sound.

The noise startled me and I looked away for a split second. When I looked back the angel and the star had gone. I tried to look hard but could only see the clouds. It was raining quite hard. I closed my eyes and burned into my eyelids was the outline of the angel; like when you close your eyes after looking at a bright light. I grabbed my bag and hastily drew the outline on a piece of paper.

I left the cemetery that day without any anger. I felt calm and at peace. I hadn't felt this comforted since my aunt had died. The stress had gone and now whenever I feel it coming back I draw a picture of my angel.

Along with wings, light features strongly in reports of angelic visions and, as you'll see in the next chapter, bright light is also a key factor in near-death experiences and visions of the afterlife. This light is a recurring image that people use to try and explain the feeling of being completely surrounded, externally and internally by angels.

Luke didn't have a near-death experience but he was still powerfully affected by the light. Here's what he saw.

Beings of Light

Things were pretty desperate for me. I wanted to study music but my dad's gambling had cost me dear. I had nowhere to live and nothing that I felt I wanted to live for. I had no friends and no money. My only option was to sign up at the YMCA for a bed for the night.

One morning I woke in a state of darkness. I was in such fear. I felt I was about to fall off a cliff. I figured the world would be a better place without me. I went to a couple of chemists and got some sleeping pills and then took them all. I thought that nobody would notice and I'd be dead before morning.

Somebody did find me and I was rushed to hospital to have my stomach pumped. When I finally came out of my coma I was hit by the blackness again. I knew that as soon as I was discharged I would take pills again but this time I'd make sure nobody found me. To get myself discharged, though, I had to be on the mend so I pretended that I wanted to get well.

As soon as I was strong enough the nurses encouraged me to have a shower. I did as I was told and within a week I was allowed to shower by myself. It was then that something incredible happened to me. I was standing in the shower looking at the little window above me with sunlight streaking through when I heard a voice inside me telling me to turn around and see the light. Gathering all the courage I could find I forced myself to turn around and was engulfed in the brightest light I could possibly imagine, but it didn't hurt my eyes at all.

It's hard to describe how I felt but love and optimism were definitely there. I knew that the darkness was leaving me and that I was turning around physically and mentally. This moment defined the rest of my life and was the beginning of a complete recovery.

Beings of light and accounts of angels appearing in all their splendour, with wings and love radiating from them can't help but arouse passion, curiosity and awe in the reader. It's small wonder that these stories often get a lot of press but in my opinion angelic visions are spectacular not because they are so dramatic but because they are reminders that angels are in all of us. More often than not, if you take away the wings and the blinding light the angel description resembles in some way the human form.

So whenever people ask me what I think a real angel looks like I always tell them to take a look at themselves in the mirror.

CHAPTER 7

Into the Light

There is an old saying that before a baby is born,
God kisses its soul. And as its guardian angel
bears it earthward to its little body, he sings. Is
there, in my subconscious self, still a dim memory
of that kiss, a faint echo of that song?

Prayer at a Greek Wedding

I saw the tracks of angels in the earth,
The beauty of heaven walking by itself on the world.

Francesco Petrarch

The expression 'Angel of Death' is one that is familiar to
us all. It often has sinister overtones. But there's a strong
suggestion by people who have had visions of the afterlife or near-death experiences when they hovered
between life and death, that 'Angel of Light' would be a
far better description. It's clear from the accounts of
people contributing to this book that angels are close by

and ready to help us into the other world when death is close. It's also clear that at the time of death angels radiate love, comfort and reassurance through bright light and their familiar form.

It's only natural to fear death, but hopefully the stories included in this chapter will help replace any fear with comfort and hope. As you will see, some of those who have glimpsed the radiant colours and deep, comforting love of the afterlife are reluctant to come back. Matthew, whose story was sent to me a few years ago by his mother, certainly wanted to return.

I Want to Go Back

This isn't my story but my son's. He was two and a half years old when he nearly drowned in my back garden. I'd blown up an inflatable paddling pool and filled it with water for my five-year-old daughter to play in. It wasn't a very big paddling pool and only went up to my daughter's knees. I thought my son was upstairs watching a DVD with his dad while I was in the living room chatting to my mum. My daughter came in asking for a biscuit and a glass of milk. I was cross with her as she was getting water all over the living room carpet. I went upstairs to get a towel and popped my head into my bedroom to say hi to the men in my life.

When I looked in I saw my husband lying on the bed but Matthew was nowhere to be seen. I asked where he was. My husband told me that he'd gone downstairs about five or ten minutes ago to ask me for a drink. He thought he was with me. I felt sick to my stomach. Immediately I ran outside to the pool and found Matthew floating face down with his upper body beginning to sink. My husband ran out with me too and we both let out a wail and pulled him out of the water. My mother called 999. I was in a state of shock. My son, my brilliant and beautiful son was turning blue and his lips were green and purple.

I'm not an expert in first aid or anything but I could tell he wasn't breathing and this was deadly dangerous. I cursed the fact that neither my husband nor I knew how to perform mouth-to-mouth or CPR. We made some futile attempts, remembering what we had seen on medical soap operas but neither of us knew what we were doing. Our son was dying in our arms and it was our fault. I started to babble hysterically. I wanted the world to swallow me whole.

Even though we thought we weren't helping we must have been doing some good because after about five minutes Matthew coughed up some water. It landed on my face and I have never been so happy to see vomit in my life. He was breathing. The paramedics arrived moments later and rushed him into hospital. I sat with him holding his hand, willing him to live. He lost consciousness again but the paramedics revived him. The five-minute drive to the hospital seemed like an eternity. I was totally freaking out at this point and trying to give him constant mouth-to-mouth. One of the paramedics had to restrain me as the ambulance flew along at breakneck speed.

When we arrived at the hospital he was rushed into casualty. I was asked a lot of questions, one of them being how long he was in the water, as they were worried about brain damage. It could have been one minute or ten. I told them that I had no idea.

Matthew was kept in the hospital for two nights for observation but mercifully he wasn't permanently damaged in any way by his near drowning. There isn't a day that goes by that I'm not grateful for that blessing. When we got back home after the ordeal it was another bright, sunny day. Matthew immediately asked if he could go into the pool again. Obviously, I told him that it was out of the question. I asked my husband to throw the pool away. I never wanted to see it again but Matthew just burst into tears. Over the next few days he was mighty persistent about the pool.

'I want pool. Give me pool,' he kept saying. Eventually, my mother told us that it might be a good idea to buy another pool and to sit with him when he played in it. 'If he's not afraid we shouldn't be afraid,' she told me. I didn't want my son growing up afraid of having fun and fearful of drowning every time he was near water so I agreed. We bought him a new pool.

Matthew squealed with delight when my husband pumped up the new paddling pool. He stripped down to his underwear and jumped right in. I was shocked and ran over but he was fine. He even put his head under water several times. I couldn't believe how confident he was in the water. He seemed happy splashing around, and watching him filled my heart with joy. I wasn't going to take my eyes off him for a second.

Later that evening as we sat watching TV Matthew suddenly started to cry. He cried so hard his eyes were red and it was hard for him to breathe. I called my husband and we thought about calling the hospital but my husband thought it might be better for us first to find out what was wrong. I picked him up and gently rocked him and when the sobbing eased I asked him what the matter was. Then he sobbed out quietly, 'I want to fly with the angels again. I want to see grandpa again. I couldn't find them in the pool.' My heart stopped. I had read about near-death experiences in books but I didn't know anyone who had had one and here I was with my little son telling me he wanted to see angels again.

I asked Matthew to tell me what he remembered. He told me in broken sentences that he had wanted to fish a stone out of the bottom of the paddling pool because it glittered but he had fallen over. He said he had tried to get his head out of the water but there were lots of stones and insects down there. He said that he saw white light all around him and then he saw grandpa Alex who told him his mum needed him to go back. Then he said he saw me acting crazy when I pulled him out of the water. He also told me that he remembered the ambulance because he'd seen the white light and the people with wings again when he was in it.

My dad died when my son was about one year old so I don't know how he knew him; although I had shown him pictures in the family album. When I asked my son to describe his grandpa he didn't describe him as he was in any of the pictures around the house. He described him as having a full set of hair and a cigar in his mouth. My dad went bald when I was a young child and I didn't have any photos of him when he was young. I certainly didn't have any photos of him smoking as one of the first things he did when I was born was to stop smoking.

My son is nearly ten now and he doesn't remember any of what happened. He's a brilliant swimmer, though, and has just qualified for the national swimming squad. Considering that I'm a weak swimmer and my husband hates putting his head under water I have no idea where that talent comes from but I'm not surprised. Nothing surprises me any more because I know that miracles can and do happen – my son is walking proof.

If his mother and father hadn't pulled him out in time Matthew wouldn't be alive today. Although it is hard to question the validity of a three year old's angel description, what he experienced sounds very much like a near-death experience or NDE.

Near-Death Experiences

NDEs are mystical experiences that tend to occur when a person is either clinically dead, or in a state where death is imminent. NDEs are common enough that they have entered our everyday language. Phrases like, 'my life flashed before my eyes,' and 'go to the light,' come from decades of research into mystical experiences which people have when they are at the brink of death.

Dr Raymond Moody coined the term near-death experience in his 1975 book, *Life After Life*, although reports of such experiences have occurred throughout history. For instance, way back in time Plato's *Republic*, written in 360 BCE, contains the tale of a soldier named Er who had an NDE after being killed in battle but returned to his mortal body days later to tell his story.

While there are doubts about NDEs, one thing is certain. They do exist. Thousands of people from all over the world report similar sensations when they are close to death. NDEs don't follow a pattern but they do often share the following similar traits. First, there is a feeling of calmness and acceptance followed by intense, pure, bright light that fills the room. The person may feel disassociated from their body in some way. They can look down and see it, often describing the sight of doctors working on it. Many NDE subjects find themselves in a tunnel with a light at its end. They may encounter spirit beings and angels as they pass through the tunnel. There may be some form of communication with a spirit being, usually the spirit of a loved one who has passed. This is often expressed as a strong voice telling them that it is not their time and to go back to their body. Some subjects report being told to choose between going into the light or returning to their earthly body. There may also be a life review when the subject sees his or her entire life in a flashback.

Reading what people have seen, felt and learned during near-death experiences can be very beneficial because their stories encourage thoughtful living and show that life doesn't end with death. Rana's story is a good example of how an NDE offers hope, comfort and encouragement.

Valentine's Day

It was 14 February, 1989. I was 23 and I'd just been dumped by my boyfriend – on Valentine's Day of all days! I was crazy with anger and grief. My heart was broken.

I took the day off work because I knew I'd be bursting into tears all the time. I spent most of the day wandering around aimlessly, fighting back tears. I didn't eat or drink. I just walked and walked for hour after hour.

The car was travelling at 45 miles an hour in a 30-mile speed limit when it hit me. If I hadn't been so numb with grief I might have noticed it and reacted quickly enough before it ran me over. My skull was crushed. I could feel my face swelling fast, and I could see in two different directions.

Someone yelled, 'Call an ambulance.' It seemed like only seconds and the ambulance was there. In the ambulance they started an IV and rushed me to the hospital. We went in through emergency, and straight up to the operating room. Lying on the table, I saw the nurses and doctors with their backs to me readying for the operation ahead. Then this strange feeling came over me, and I told myself, 'Robin, you can just stop breathing.'

With a sudden whoosh, it was like I was on a super-fast elevator going up through a tunnel. Ahead was only darkness, when suddenly there was a very bright light far away but straight ahead of me. Then I felt a sudden stop and I had this overwhelming feeling of total knowledge of everything that had ever happened, and everything that ever will happen. Every question I ever had in my life was suddenly answered. There was an intense smell, like the most fragrant garden imaginable. I heard (or felt) a voice saying, 'Robin, you know what's happening to you, don't you?' I said, 'Yes, grandma. I'm dying.' She then said to me, 'You shouldn't be dying. You have so much to do.' I told her, 'I can't live without him,' and my grandma nodded and smiled at me, saying, 'You're strong without him.' She then told me to stop looking at the light.

I turned away from the light. I felt myself falling fast but gently down. It's strange, but I could actually feel my mother's love pulling me back to earth (even though she had no idea what was happening to me). I opened my eyes, and heard a nurse say, 'Doctor, she's breathing.'

I was in hospital for six months and had several operations to rebuild my face but it wasn't just my face that was rebuilt after the accident; my heart was too. I'd always doubted my ability to cope alone but the angels had strengthened me. Each time I feel that life is tough, I go back to that moment when my grandma smiled and nodded to me and reminded me of my own strength. Yes, the old me died on that operating table, but a stronger me was reborn.

Although near-death experiences tend to occur when a person is in danger of losing their life, you don't necessarily have to be close to death to experience a life-changing vision of the afterlife, as Becky's story illustrates.

The Golden Place

I'd just given birth to twins and I was exhausted. I lost a lot of blood during delivery and had stayed in hospital for a month after the birth. This was my first day home on my own with them and I was tired and scared. The twins had barely settled into a regular napping routine and I didn't know whether I was coming or going. My mum had visited in the morning but this afternoon I was alone and it was all down to me.

I'd longed to have children but nothing prepares you for the reality of having them, and here I was with two helpless creatures dependent on me. I didn't feel that I could cope or that I was a good enough mum. I'd already made a hash of breastfeeding and my decision not to breastfeed had clearly disappointed the midwives. In truth I felt disappointed with myself. I wasn't bonding as well as I had hoped.

Anyway, I fed them both some formula and put them down for an afternoon nap. Miraculously, they both nodded off at the same time and I leapt at the chance to put my feet up. I knew I had to doze lightly so that I could hear them if they woke and needed me but this nap would prove quite different to any nap I have had before or since.

I must have been so exhausted that I fell into a deep sleep right away. In a flash I felt myself falling down a deep, dark hole. I looked down and saw a dim light growing brighter and brighter. And then I felt myself falling into a different place. I looked around, and everything was white and gold. I was standing in a street which was paved with gold bricks, with high walls that were white and smooth. I thought I was walking, but I didn't seem to be moving. It was as if the scenery was rolling by me.

Someone seemed to be there, I felt their presence, but just could not see them. The sun was stunningly bright. There was a brilliant sparkle about everything. I had to shield my eyes to avoid the glare. Suddenly, I noticed a man on the other side of the street. He wore a long, flowing golden robe, and he was tall and very well built. As I followed the outline of his clothing, I suddenly realized that what I at first thought was some kind of hood on his robe was actually a pair of golden wings. The thought crossed my mind that I was seeing a real angel, a beautiful creature so much like a man, yet physically perfect. I was admiring his shining blonde hair that was like spun gold, when he turned his head and looked at me.

His face was perfect, his skin smooth and golden and his eyes were like blue crystal sapphires. He glided toward me. He was smiling and pleased to see me, almost as if he had been expecting me and was waiting on the street for me to arrive. As he approached me I felt empowered, happy and full of energy. Without speaking audibly, he imparted to me these words: 'You are a wonderful mother and there are wonderful things ahead for you.'

Suddenly, I felt drawn back to the darkness. I opened my eyes and I was on my couch again. I looked around because I could still sense the golden man with me. I felt him step back from me and then he was gone. I felt so excited. I knew that this had not been a dream. It had been real. I looked over at the clock and it was about 7 pm. I had slept for more than three hours.

Panicking, I jumped from my couch to check on the twins. When I got to their cot they were both sound asleep. They had never slept that long before. Gently I woke them up. I didn't fully realize until a few days later that from that moment I had more energy than before. And I stopped feeling frightened of my children and started enjoying loving them.

I've never been to church in my life and I've never thought that much about angels until now, but somehow I know that this being infused me with hope and healing. I was in danger of slipping into severe post-natal depression and it was a turning point. I still don't know what 'wonderful things' lie ahead for me to do but being a happy, healthy mum surely must be one of them.

Becky mentions in her account that her experience was a turning point in her life. Nigel, who tells his story below, also feels that his vision of the afterlife was a blessing in disguise.

Rewind

For several months I'd suffered from severe pain in my chest and arms and foolishly I didn't go and see the doctor. I'd just turned 30 and didn't think I was a candidate for a heart attack. I was fit and healthy and led a crazy, fun-filled life. I had the car, the job, the money and the lifestyle. Sadly, my love of the bachelor lifestyle cost me my marriage. I had an affair and my wife divorced me after two years. We had a daughter and she went to live with her mum. I saw her once or twice a month, but didn't really feel I was cut out for fatherhood.

I was just recovering from a bout of flu when a friend asked me to play a game of squash. Foolishly I agreed, and after two games I was lying on the floor in the middle of the squash courts having a savage heart attack.

I must have lost consciousness. I felt drawn through a dark tunnel with light at the end. When I reached it, I was surrounded by light beings; many had faces or shapes. One light figure started talking to me and told me not to be afraid, that he was an angel. He told me the angels would appear to me both in physical forms and in light bodies, showing me so I would not be afraid. He told me that I would be sent back because there was a special plan for me and this would be revealed to me later. I was not afraid, for the warmth of the light and the light bodies around me was full of love, giving me a sense of security.

Suddenly I was back in my body but I couldn't open my eyes. I saw paramedics put me on a stretcher and bundle me into an ambulance. I saw them trying to revive me.

Then I remember being surrounded by bright lights. I felt so happy. I remembered everything about my life from the very first spark. I relived every tear, every sigh and every kiss. I remembered what my purpose was on earth. I remember wondering why I spent so much of my time on earth on things that didn't matter.

I don't remember much else, except that I was filled with joy and happiness. I didn't want to leave but I knew that I had to go back. Then I saw my daughter crying because once again I'd cancelled my weekend with her due to work commitments. I asked the angels if she was okay and they said she was fine but she was upset with me. I could feel her hurt, her loss.

In the next moment I was back in the in hospital. I felt my body filling with warm, intense light and then it was gone. The feeling was so intense and full of love that I felt safe and secure. I opened my eyes and a doctor asked me if I was okay.

I learned a lot that day about life and death. The angels touched and enriched my soul. I see my daughter twice a week now and am learning to be a better dad. I'm no expert but my experience showed me that in the realm of the angels there is only love and truth and any act that is thoughtless or selfish or hurts someone else is relived.

That's why I always take a moment to reflect on my actions and words now to make sure they come from a place of love and compassion, not just for myself but for others.

Deathbed Visions

Deathbed visions differ from near-death experiences in that the person experiencing the vision doesn't typically return to life or have much longer to live and their stories are told after their death by loved ones present at the scene. Such deathbed visions are not just the stuff of stories and movies. They are, in fact, more common than you might think and, like near-death experiences, their traits are surprisingly similar across nationalities, religions and cultures. Instances of these unexplained visions have been recorded throughout history and continue to stand as one of the most compelling proofs of life after death. Take Lily's touching story, for example.

Gently Dying

My mother was breathing heavily and gently dying. Sporadically, she would open her eyes and smile at me and mumble. I couldn't hear everything she said but she told me her room was filled with glowing beings of light. They were all smiling warmly at her and beckoning her to join them. She told me she felt herself being lifted up and taken to a beautiful place where there were flowers and lush green trees. She had been bedridden for three years but in this place she could walk and dance. She felt weightless. Then the beings of light brought her back to her bed and kissed her and told her it would soon be time to go home. My mother said the angels were so tender with her and they had eyes filled with love. Their wings felt like silk and shimmered like diamonds. When they spoke they whispered.

Mum told me she wasn't afraid to die and I shouldn't be sad. She said she was going to a beautiful place when she left her body behind. A week later mum died. The last thing she said was that she saw my dad waiting for her. She held my hand and smiled and then the smile slowly faded. She let out one last breath and then her gentle death was over. Mum's courage and hope in the face of death have given me courage and hope to rebuild my life.

Anecdotes of deathbed visions have appeared in literature throughout the ages, but it wasn't until the 20th century that the subject received scientific study. What researchers have found is that whether or not the dying person believes in an afterlife, each story has remarkable consistencies. For example, the vast majority claim to see beings of light or familiar people who have previously passed away. The dying person is reassured by the experience and expresses great happiness with the vision and their mood – even their state of health – seems to change. During these visions, a once depressed or pain-riddled person is overcome with elation and momentarily relieved of pain. And finally, the dying person does not seem to be hallucinating or in an altered state of consciousness due to medication; rather, they continue to be lucid and aware of their real surroundings and conditions.

All the evidence suggests to me that deathbed visions are exactly what they appear to be: a welcoming committee of angels who have come to ease the transition to life on another plane of existence. And, most comforting of all, these powerful visions dramatically lessen or completely remove the patients' fear of dying and are enormously healing to the relatives.

It is my firm belief that reading about near-death experiences and deathbed visions can help change our overall attitude to death. Many of us fear it and find it hard to handle the passing of a loved one. If, however, we can recognize that death is nothing to be afraid of, it can help us live our lives more fully.

I'll leave the last word to Benjamin, who had a near-death experience three years ago. He has since passed away, but his story and his spirit lives on.

Was It Worth Dying?

From the corner of the room I could see emergency medical staff crowding around an unconscious body. They were desperately trying to revive a man. In an instant I knew that it was me they were trying to revive and it made total sense to me that I should be watching my own death.

Since I was in a coma I have no idea when my near-death experience occurred, but from reading my medical charts I'm guessing it must have been Christmas Eve, 1999. Apparently I 'died' from massive internal bleeding. I'm a firefighter. Falling debris had knocked me off my ladder and I fell about 30 feet, crushing the bones in my body. My relatives were told to prepare for the worst. My body was shutting down and a ventilator was keeping me 'alive'.

Watching my final moments wasn't terrifying. It didn't feel weird. It felt perfectly natural. I felt peaceful and serene. I was aware of a bright light swirling around me, lifting me. The light became so intense that I couldn't see my unconscious body any more. Then I felt as if the light was rushing towards me or perhaps I was rushing towards it.

I felt myself floating higher and higher. I became pure thought and pure feeling. From my high point I just had to think of a place or person or time and I was there, witnessing everything. I went back to witness my own birth. I saw my sons being born. I went on my first date. I don't know why but I felt a strong pull towards Canada, even though I've never been there before in my life. Well, suddenly I was there flying over Niagara Falls and floating over the purple mountains. All I had done was think about somewhere I had always wanted to visit but hadn't and I was there.

Starting to enjoy this I thought of a sandy beach and the sun beating down on me. I was there. Then I thought of the moon. I was an astronaut taking 'one small step for man but a giant leap for mankind'. Every place I visited – and there were hundreds – was comforting and bright. I was everywhere, everything and everyone. I became the world and every person in it. I had no 'body' that I could touch or feel. There was nothing to drag me down or contain me. The feeling was liberating and euphoric and went on for seconds or for trillions of years. I didn't have a clue as time didn't exist any more and didn't have any meaning or relevance to me. My feelings were of comfort, peace, awe and a sense of naturalness, but the strongest feeling of all was of love, although the word love seems inadequate to describe the depth, breadth and intensity of my heart.

This eruption of emotion and overpowering love – which words again fail to describe fully – was all the time pushing me upwards so I could observe, absorb and become more. I'd moved beyond the world into the solar system and the universe. We are not alone in this

Universe. It seemed as if all the creations in the Universe soared past me and vanished in a speck of light. I could feel my world flashing past me and then vanishing into light. And still I kept moving upwards. I saw hundreds of other universes rotating around a void of light.

That light was the most beautiful thing I have ever seen. It was like all the love you've ever wanted, and it was the kind of love that cures, heals, regenerates. At that instant the truth was obvious to me that regardless of race and religion we are connected. I could see that there is no death and nothing is born and nothing dies; we are immortal beings, part of a natural living system that recycles itself endlessly. The pull towards the light was strong. I was melting into the light. I longed to merge with it but I never made it.

I couldn't see him, but I knew that my father, who had died six years previously, was there with me, and I felt totally, totally safe. I felt that he was almost carrying me, like I was a child again, and then the light slowed and stopped and my father told me that it wasn't my time yet. I felt very sad that I had to leave, but I wanted to be with my family. There was another instant where I was still surrounded by light, and then, bang! I slammed backwards.

My vision had ended. I was back in my body.

I drifted in and out of a coma for some time after that; I have no idea of how long. I believe I probably experienced death itself for at least an hour and a half. When

I recovered, I was surprised and awed about what had happened. I kept slipping out of this world and kept asking, 'Am I alive?' This world seemed more like a dream than that one.

The doctors could not believe that I had survived. Within a week I was feeling normal again, clearer, yet different than ever before. My memories of the journey I had taken when I was in the coma started to filter back. I could find nothing wrong with any human being I had ever seen. I thought of myself as a human again and I was happy to be that. From what I have seen, I would be happy to be an atom in this universe. I'm aware that a lot of what I've been saying doesn't sound logical or reasonable but I've seen that logic and reason, along with time and separation and differences between people, are illusions. They aren't real. I knew that what I had experienced wasn't a hallucination or a dream. It had been real. I knew that the only thing that matters and is completely real is love. Complete, open, giving and incredibly filling love. That is the only thing that matters. All else is superfluous.

I'm fully aware that my story sounds 'trippy' to say the least. I would have dismissed it as a hallucination before it happened to me so I completely understand if you don't believe me. I just want you to know that before it happened I'd never been religious or spiritual and I didn't talk to angels, but after my vision I was changed forever.

I simply am changed. We are all one. We are the world, the universe, the angels and God. I'm no expert but from what I've since read and heard about near-death experiences, although people may describe what they have 'seen' in their own religious terminology, religion is immaterial. The central message is of universal and uniting love: regardless of where you were born and which God you worship, we are all one. I now find myself openly crying over the sadness in the world and in people's lives. If I can somehow relieve another's suffering by sharing it with them I will do so gladly. But I also find myself rejoicing whenever there is joy and laughter in the world.

Above all, though, I share the same feeling about death that others who have experienced similar near-death experiences have – a total lack of fear. It's comforting and warming to know where I will be heading. I feel like I've had a sneak preview. Six months ago I was diagnosed with lung cancer. I'm not afraid. I'm living fully and loving every second of my life, right now. I don't know how long I have to live but ever since I went over to the other side with a lot of fear about death I have come back loving death as much as my life, and all the problems in it.

In a nutshell, I suppose the question many people want to ask me would be, 'Was it worth dying?' I would have to answer joyfully, 'Yes!'

CHAPTER 8

Angels are all Around

Millions of spiritual creatures walk the
earth Unseen, both when we wake and
when we sleep.

John Milton, *Paradise Lost*

When you see God's hand in everything, it is easy
to leave everything in God's hands.

Anon

I hope all the stories in this book have helped you see
that you don't need to be a saint, a prophet, a mystic or a
celebrity medium to see and hear angels. Most of the
accounts here are from ordinary people leading normal
lives. Some of these people already had a firm belief in
angels making them more open to the experience, but
many others didn't. Some of the experiences were triggered by a crisis or threat of some sort, but others
happened for no apparent reason.

Whether or not you think you have seen or heard an angel, what matters most is how much you are prepared to open your mind to the possibility of the miraculous. This matters because if you are prepared to accept that logic cannot explain everything, and allow a little magic and mystery into your life, you are far more likely to see subtle signs from the afterlife all around you. You are far more likely to hear the voice of your guardian angel.

I haven't distinguished between the voice of your guardian angel and the voice of your intuition because the two are so strongly connected that it is often hard to tell the difference. Like a caller put on hold with crucial information to offer you, your intuition already knows the answers to your problems – you just need to renew the connection and start listening again. Some people will hear voices, others will see images, and still others will be guided by their gut feelings, but whatever way your guardian angel chooses to speak to you, rest assured that the same miraculous process is at work.

What I'm trying to say here is that everyone can hear the voice of their guardian angel, if they take the time and find the stillness within them to listen. But our guardian angels won't be able to help us if we don't learn to quieten the noisy chatter in our minds and get in touch with the positive, loving, compassionate or, if you prefer, 'angelic' aspect of ourselves. When you ask your guardian angel for help you must do so from a still place within yourself of love, trust, humility and clarity. As long as your request is positive and does not interfere with anyone else's wellbeing and your life plan, then rest assured, your guardian angel will answer your call.

Angels are all around us, all the time, in the air we breathe. Once you can get in touch with your inner self you can tune into their frequency and hear their words, either spoken aloud or in your mind. So, welcome angels into your life, talk to them and give thanks for their endless love and wisdom. And when you do hear an angel call your name, listen very carefully. It might just transform your life, like it changed mine and those of many of the people who contributed their experiences for this book.

An Unexpected End

It's been a remarkable journey for me writing this book. Initially, I thought it would be a fairly straightforward process of collecting inspiring and positive stories of extraordinary occurrences that happen to ordinary people. My task was simply to gather the stories and pull them together but as soon as I started listening, reading, interviewing and writing I realized that it was going to be something much bigger than that. Every story that I was sent, read or heard moved me deeply. I agonized not only over which stories to select but also how to do them justice. All of them were astonishing and awe-inspiring in their own way. Every story taught me something profound.

Before starting this book I'd got so caught up in work, routine and life that there never seemed enough time in my life for anything or anyone, with constant deadlines to meet and endless things to do. I got so busy and absent minded at times that I'd do daft things like forgetting to put my shoes on when I went shopping and only realizing I had my slippers on at the checkout.

Thankfully, the stories here helped remind me of something I instinctively knew as a child but had forgotten somewhere along the line: how awe-inspiring the world we live in is and how precious every moment of life is. And every time my perspective shifted from one of stress and haste to one of gratitude and clarity something miraculous happened: the stories started to write themselves. The time that I didn't think I had for getting organized and for laughter somehow appeared. The more attention I paid to my guardian angel, the more guided, inspired, loved and blessed I felt.

Angels want us to know that we need never feel alone. Their destiny is to love and support us in all that we do so that we can have the lives we all deserve. Their purpose is to inspire us to see the astonishing miracles and limitless possibilities all around us every precious moment of our lives.

William Blake, the English poet who saw and heard angels all his life, famously saw the world in a grain of sand, so why not see an angel in a grain of sand, a raindrop, a sunset, a white feather, a passing cloud, the warmth of a hug, the magic of coincidences and answered prayers, or anything else that inspires and comforts you? Why not hear an angel call your name in the soft breeze, in a bird's song, in the voices of people you love, in your conscience or in your dreams?

Why not let these angel stories work a miracle inside you and help you see the universe as it truly is: a place of unexpected wonder?

I'll leave you, for now, with one of my favourite angel blessings:

Angels around us, angels beside us, angels within us.
Angels are watching over you when times are good or
    stressed.
Their wings wrap gently around you,
Whispering you are loved and blessed.